Drunk On You

A LOVE & WHISKEY NOVEL

USA TODAY BESTSELLING AUTHOR
NIKKI ASH

I'm just getting started,
and I'm already drunk on her.

Drunk on You Playlist

Undrunk – Fletcher
Beautiful – Akon
I Feel it Coming – The Weeknd
Crazy – K.C. & JoJo
Future Ex – Abigail Barlow & Ariza
Last Night – Morgan Wallen
Don't – Ed Sheeran
U Got it Bad – Usher
Yeah! – Usher
There's Nothing Holding Me Back – Shawn Mendes

To the women who are struggling to find their place in this world, you aren't alone.

I see you. I believe in you. You got this.

One

ANASTASIA

"Thank you, *Annabella*. That will be all," Victoria says, closing the file folder we were just going over and sitting back in her seat.

With her half-black, half-silver hair, she reminds me of Cruella de Vil from *101 Dalmatians*, and I briefly wonder if she has a stash of puppies she's holding hostage somewhere.

"It's Anastasia," I correct, not for the first time, as I pick up the reports off the table. "If there's anything else you—"

"Nope. I think we have everything we need." She plasters on a fake smile, silently indicating I've been dismissed.

I stuff the files into my Bottega Veneta briefcase that my father sent me for my birthday last year and then stand, feeling completely rejected. I spent hours upon hours working on those reports and projections, only for *Cruella* to barely give them a glance. When I'd brought up the idea at a meeting last month and she said I was welcome to pitch it, I should've known she was full of shit.

When I get back to my office, Paige—my best friend and colleague—is waiting for me. Between her slim figure, stunning looks, and the fact that, with heels on, she towers over most men, she looks more like a runway model than a marketing executive for Benson Liquor. The second she sees my facial expression, her pouty lips turn down.

"Such a damn waste," I hiss once my door is closed.

I fish the files out of my bag and toss them into the garbage can, annoyed that I wasted so much of my time working on them when I knew Victoria didn't care about anyone's opinions or ideas but her own. I round my desk and slump back into my seat while Paige takes a seat in the visitor chair across from me.

"It's not you," she says, blowing wisps of her blonde hair out of her eyes. "Victoria is a controlling know-it-all, and if she keeps it up, she's going to run this company straight into the ground."

She's not lying. The numbers are down thirty percent for the quarter—an all-time low for the company. Victoria is blaming it on the economy, but when you compare our numbers to our competitors', theirs have gone up. The economy might be on shaky ground right now, but that isn't stopping people from drinking.

"And the last thing I want is to be here when it happens." I clasp my hands over my stomach and cross my legs. "I'll never understand why her father thought it was a good idea to let his socialite daughter, who knows nothing about the liquor industry, take over the company when he retired."

"Because she's a daddy's girl," Paige mocks and then gags, making me choke out a laugh despite not being in a laughing mood.

"Must be nice," I mutter just as my phone rings with *Dad* on my screen. "And speak of the devil ..."

I turn my phone so Paige can see, and she flinches.

"You sure you want to answer that? You've already had a bad enough morning."

"Better to get the conversation over with."

She nods in understanding and stands. "Lunch?"

"You're not meeting John?" Since Paige and her boyfriend work near each other, they usually meet for lunch.

"Nope, he has a lunch meeting."

"Okay, then let's do lunch."

"Sounds good."

Since I missed my dad's call, I call him back once Paige has closed the door behind her.

"Anastasia, have I caught you at a bad time?" he asks when he answers.

"I'm at work, but I have a few minutes."

Dad sighs at my curtness, and I close my eyes, hating what's become of us.

I would give anything to have a relationship with the only parent I have left, but it's hard to do when that parent is partially responsible for the death of my other parent.

When I was little, I was close to my dad—well, as close as I could be as the daughter of a workaholic—but the bigger his business grew, the more he put it above his family. I tried everything to get his attention, including acting out and getting into some trouble in my teens, but my mom and I just couldn't compete with his company.

After I graduated from high school and left for college, things between my parents only got worse, especially when I continued to lash out and damn near failed out of college my freshman year. Luckily, I turned it around and got my life together before it was too late.

Just before my college graduation, Mom asked him for a divorce, but he begged her to give him another chance, swearing things would be different. Of course, she agreed—because he was the only man she'd ever loved—but while they were at dinner a couple of weeks after my graduation, he proved tigers couldn't change their stripes. I don't know all the details, but from what he said, there was an issue that came up with work that he had to deal with. She got annoyed that he was ignoring her by texting and taking calls during their meal, and she stormed out of the restaurant.

As she stepped onto the sidewalk, a car came out of nowhere—a drunk driver who lost control and barreled right up onto the sidewalk—and hit her. Dad was behind her and saw the entire thing. He called 911 and held her in his arms, but she died before they made it there.

After losing my mom, who had also been my best friend, I took off to England, got my MBA in hospitality, and went to work for Benson Liquor, becoming one of their lead marketing analysts.

My dad and I didn't speak for several years—not for his lack of trying—but on the third anniversary of Mom's death, he left me a message, begging to talk. So, I gave in.

It's been three years, and we usually talk once or twice a month. I hate the distance between us, and I know my dad isn't the one who killed her, but a part of me can't help but blame him.

"And how is work?" Dad asks conversationally.

"Busy," I say back. "You know, trying to create a future for myself." I can't keep the bitterness out of my tone.

I'm exhausted. I've been working sixty-plus hours a week for the past several years, hoping to work my way up the corporate ladder. I always thought I'd end up working with my dad, but after everything went down and I left, he never once asked me to come home and work for his company. Hell, he won't even discuss business with me.

"I don't want to mix business with family," is what he says anytime I bring up anything business related.

Whenever anyone asks, he always says he misses me but is proud of me for spreading my wings and flying.

"Life's too short," he says, making me roll my eyes. "You should focus on finding happiness."

This isn't the first time he's said this, but today, after I had to deal with Victoria, his words hit harder.

"Says the man who was married to his work," I mutter.

"Exactly," he agrees. "Which means I know what it's like to give something your everything and lose everyone that matters because of it."

A lump of emotion lodges in my throat at his admittance, but I manage to swallow it down. He made his decisions, and now, we all have to live with them.

"Speaking of which," he adds when I don't say anything in return, "Selene and I are hosting Thanksgiving this year. I know it's quite a few months away, but I was hoping with enough notice, you could put in for time off and come visit. I can pay for your flight."

Selene is his new wife. They met a little over a year ago, and within six months, they were married. I have nothing against her—I haven't even met her yet—but the thought of getting to know her feels like I would be betraying my mom.

"You know I can pay for my own flight."

I make a decent living, working at Benson—even if Victoria won't listen to a word I have to say. But even if I didn't, I'm worth millions, thanks to the money and assets left to me from my mom when she died and the trust my dad set up for me. But I've never touched the money he gave me. I feel like if I do, then I have to completely let him back in, and I'm just not ready to do that yet.

"I know," he murmurs. "It's just … I miss you, Anastasia. And I'd love for you to meet Selene. What if we came to you?"

"I can't," I choke out. "Work is busy during that time. Maybe after the first of the year. I have to go."

Without waiting for him to respond, I click End on the call and throw my phone on the desk. Then, with my face in my hands, I let out a cathartic sob, allowing myself a moment of vulnerability before I slip my shield back on.

"So, any chance of you moving back to Texas?" Paige asks just before she snatches up a piece of sushi and pops it into her mouth.

"And why would I do that?" I ask, taking a bite of my food.

Once she's done chewing, she washes it down with a sip of sake and then leans in. "Um, because the owner and CEO of Kingston Limited, who just so happens to be your father, has announced he's retiring at the end of the year. I figured that was why he called you."

Despite choosing to use my mother's maiden name, Webb, so I wouldn't have people thinking I was using his name to get further in the business world, I've allowed one person to know who I really am—Paige. It took a while before I completely let her in, but I knew she'd never tell a soul.

"He what?" I gasp, having no damn clue what she's talking about.

"He didn't tell you?" Her brows pinch together in confusion.

"No! Are you sure?"

The man I know would never step down. He lives and breathes Kingston Limited.

I pull my phone out and do a search, and sure enough, the first article that pops up is about him announcing his retirement. As I scan the words, I can't believe what I'm seeing, but more than that ...

"He didn't tell me," I whisper, trying and failing to tamp down my emotions.

According to this article, before he retires, he'll be appointing a new CEO to take his place and run Kingston Limited.

Paige's features soften, but I don't want her sympathy. What I want is to know why my father wouldn't even mention to his daughter, who grew up in the liquor industry and has worked in it for years, that he's stepping down.

"I need to get out of here," I tell her, standing abruptly.

"Go. I've got this," she says.

"Thanks," I mutter, slinging my purse over my shoulder and then stalking out of the restaurant.

Instead of going back to work, I head straight home, not even bothering to let anyone know.

Once I'm there, I waste no time in calling my dad, who answers on the first ring.

"Anastasia, is everything okay?"

Of course he'd ask that. Because I haven't called him since my mom passed away—he's always the one who reaches out.

"Why didn't you tell me that you're stepping down?" I ask, getting straight to the point.

"We never discuss business."

"By your choice!"

"Yes, because that business destroyed my family. Why would I talk about it when we could be talking about you? Working on our relationship?"

"That *business* is you," I point out. "When I was a little girl, I practically grew up there. I used to hang out in the conference rooms and pretend I was an employee. The only reason I stopped going was because you stopped paying attention to me."

"Anastasia," he breathes. "I'm sor—"

"Is it because you think I'm incapable?" I ask, cutting him off. "I have a degree in business! An MBA! I've lived and breathed the liquor industry my entire life. Why?" I cry out, realizing how hurt I am by his actions. "Why am I not good enough to work for Kingston?"

"No, Anastasia, that's not it," Dad says, sounding almost choked up. "I didn't even think you'd want to work for me. You ran across the pond six years ago, and

I haven't seen you since. I can't even convince you to come home to visit. But also ..." He clears his throat. "And please don't take this the wrong way, but I'm not sure you'd be a good fit as CEO of Kingston."

"What? Why?" I ask, taken aback by the change in direction of the conversation.

"Despite the issues we've had over the years, I've made it a point to portray myself as a family man. People judge liquor companies. And because of that, I feel it's best I hire someone who's more family oriented."

I can't help the scoff that bursts out.

"I know," Dad says. "I was great at being the face of the company, but not so great at the behind the scenes. And because of that, I want to make some changes. I'd like to see the company go in a different direction. Picnics, family-friendly events, maternity leave. Selene suggested putting in a day care for the employees who have babies that aren't school age.

"I'm hoping to hire someone who has a family and can help with this transition. I don't want whoever takes my place to make the same mistakes I made. To put the business above his or her family. And if I were to hire you, I fear you wouldn't find love. You'd be too busy trying to take the company to the next level, and I want more for you, Anastasia."

Who is this man, and what has he done with my dad?

"So, let me get this straight. Because you didn't put your family first, you want to make the business more family oriented, which means not hiring your own flesh and blood?"

"I'm trying to right my wrongs."

"By pushing me away?!"

"That's not what I'm doing, Anastasia. I have no doubt you're capable of running the company, but I don't think you're in the right position to run Kingston. I see so much of me in you."

"You barely know me!"

"Just because I haven't seen you doesn't mean I don't know you," he says. "You're just as business and power driven as I was."

Did he seriously just say *was*, as if he's no longer that way?

"Do you even date?" he asks. "When's the last time you did anything for yourself? I'm sorry, Anastasia, but I don't feel like hiring you would be what's best for the company. But that doesn't mean I don't love you and want a better relationship with you."

"I gotta go," I choke out, unable to listen to another word he has to say.

I vaguely hear him say my name as I click End and fling my phone across the table.

"He won't hire you because you don't have a family?" Paige's brows furrow in confusion.

"He's decided that to fix the mistakes of his past, he's going to reinvent Kingston, starting with hiring a family man ... or woman, I guess."

I pace my office, my brain and emotions running wild. I've been in this state ever since my dad and I hung up last night. I never thought I'd be so upset over him not wanting me to work there.

Dad wasn't lying when he said it destroyed our family. It might've been his decisions that landed us where we are, but it was his love of that company that made it so easy for him to choose business over his family. And I've spent the better part of my adulthood resenting both him and the company because of it.

But knowing that the spot is available—that he thinks I'm so power hungry, I'd make the same horrible mistakes he's made regarding his family—is driving me insane and making me want to prove him wrong.

And if I'm honest, a part of me wants him to see that I'm capable and make him proud.

"If I were married, I wouldn't need to reinvent the company," I scoff. "Unlike my father, I know how to manage my time. I could easily be a wife and a mom and run the company, and I wouldn't destroy everyone in my wake."

But even as I say the words out loud, I wonder if I'm telling the truth. I've worked sixty-plus-hour workweeks for as long as I can remember. Could I have accomplished what I have if I'd had to cut back the hours? If I'd had a husband and child who needed my attention?

I swallow thickly, suddenly questioning if I've been too hard on my dad. Could he have built his company to be just as successful if he had cut his hours in half? I'm not so sure. But what I do know is that it doesn't matter because what's done is done and I'm not married, nor am I having children anytime soon—if ever. And I'm definitely capable of being CEO, even as a single woman. We live in the twenty-first century, for crying out loud. I don't need a husband and two-point-five kids to successfully run a company. The problem is, once my dad is set in his ways, there's no changing his mind. Which means—

"Too bad you aren't married," Paige says with a laugh, bringing me back into the now. "Or a mom. Then, you could show him how it's done."

My eyes snap to hers. "But what if I was?"

"A mom?"

"No." I shake my head. "A wife." The craziest idea hits me. "What if I *fell in love* and got married? Then, he'd be forced to consider me for the position." And then I could show him that I'm capable of being the face of Kingston despite not being a family woman.

"You're not even dating anyone though," she points out. "And have you ever been in love?"

Ignoring her question, my brain formulates a plan. "What was that site that Ronald in advertising mentioned? The one where wealthy men can find themselves a trophy wife?"

Paige laughs. "Um, in case you haven't noticed, you're not exactly trophy-wife material. I mean, you're gorgeous, but I'm pretty sure they're also supposed to be brainless and docile."

"True, but that site has men who are used to dealing with wealth, who wouldn't blink twice at a prenup. If I could score myself one of those men, I could use him to get in the running for CEO, the same way he'd be using me." And then it hits me. "What if nobody picked me?"

Paige laughs. "Stop it. You're beautiful and smart, and you come from a wealthy family. You practically drip elegance. Sure, you'd have to fake being dumb, but there's no way any red-blooded male in his right mind wouldn't pick you to hang on his arm. Worst-case scenario"—Paige shrugs—"you pick up a guy at a bar and convince him to fake marry you."

The thought of having to search bars or clubs to pick up a guy and convince him to marry me for pretend makes my skin crawl. "Hopefully, there's someone from that service in Texas who's looking for a wife."

"Wait, Texas?" She frowns. "Does that mean you're moving?"

"That's where Kingston's headquarters is."

Paige's eyes go wide. "You're going to have to quit Benson."

"I know. I can't work here while trying to vie for the CEO position there."

Paige nods. "I'm going to miss you!" She flings her arms around me for a hug.

When we pull back, I swallow nervously and then say, "Looks like I'll be putting in my two weeks'," while wondering if I'm in over my head.

Can I really do this? Find a fake husband, move to Texas, and show up on my dad's front step, demanding he give me the chance to prove I'm capable of running his company.

Looks like there's only one way to find out.

"We need to find the number to that arranged-marriage service."

Two

JULIAN

Sharp nails scrape down my back, startling me awake. It takes me a second to remember where I am and who I'm with—at a hotel in Houston with a nameless woman I brought back here last night. Once I do, I stay still, hoping she'll give up and head out without me having to give the always-awkward *this is never happening again* speech.

But of course, like all the women who've come before her and who'll come after her, she doesn't get the hint, choosing to suction herself to my backside while she drags her fingers around my torso and down to my cock. When she gives it a squeeze, I roll away from her and get out of bed, not wanting her to think there's the slightest chance anything more will be happening between us.

When I picked her up at the club, I made sure she knew the deal—one night, no strings, and tomorrow, we part ways. Women always agree in the moment, hoping they'll be the one to change my mind, and then

I'm stuck being the bad guy when I make it clear there's no chance of a future.

They'll start off pouting, hoping to hit me in my feelings, and when that doesn't work, they bring on the seduction, thinking sex is the way to a man's heart. And when that still does nothing to change my mind, they'll get pissed and stomp out, spouting some bullshit about how I sucked in bed to convince themselves that walking away was their choice and not mine.

And I'll let them say it because I know the multiple orgasms they screamed out in bed the night before weren't fake, and if it were up to them, they'd latch on like the leeches they are. But that's not happening.

"Hey, sweetheart," I say because I can't for the life of me remember her name. "It's been fun, but I've got somewhere I need to be."

Her pout is instantaneous, and I internally groan, knowing it's not going to be easy to get rid of her.

An hour later—after being told I suck in bed at least three times and stopping at home to shower and change—I'm on my way to Rosemary Country Club to golf and have lunch with my boss, at his request.

Rosemary is a quaint town about thirty minutes south of Houston, so it doesn't take long to get anywhere you're going. I've lived here my entire life, but it wasn't until a few years ago that I stopped renting my small apartment and bought a home of my own in a development I'd only dreamed I could afford, growing up.

After leaving my car with the valet, I head to where I know Samuel will be waiting for me. I've only just entered the lobby when he spots me.

"Julian, thanks for coming." He shakes my hand and then pulls me in for a hug. "I hope I didn't force you to end your date early."

He smirks, and I chuckle. When I was leaving last night, I mentioned going on a date—read: picking up a random woman in the club. He told me if it rolls over to morning, then she's probably the one. If he only knew that I didn't bring her back to my place, instead opting to check in to a hotel room in Houston so there would be no chance of running into her again.

"I don't think there will be another date," I say with a shrug.

"Aww, well, don't give up on finding love. And once you do find it, don't let it go." He smiles at me, but I can feel the sadness in his tone.

Working for Samuel for as long as I have, I've watched him go through losing his wife, his daughter moving away—I never knew her personally, but he's talked about her over the years—and most recently, falling in love again. He's the smartest man I know, but he'll be the first to tell you he's made a lot of dumb choices over the years. Seeing as he privately owns a multibillion-dollar company, I'm going to bet most of his choices were smart regardless of how he feels now.

Still, I nod in agreement since I'm not about to tell him that finding love doesn't seem to be in the cards for me. It's not that I'm some man-whore playboy. I'm too busy to have a different woman in my bed every night. Hell, if I were willing to settle down, it would probably mean getting laid more often. But I've learned the hard way that it's easier said than done.

The truth is, the naive, younger me thought by my age, I'd be married with kids, but moving up the ranks in a company this size and this competitive doesn't happen while you're out looking for love.

I started off in the mailroom when I was eighteen and had no idea what I wanted to do with my life. From there, I was promoted to errand boy, getting drinks and food for the bigwigs.

But then a few years later, Samuel saw something in me and took me under his wing, helping me become the businessman I am today.

I went from the broke guy women wanted to fuck, but didn't want to settle down with because I couldn't provide for them, to the millionaire that women only want for my money.

There is one other option—the wealthy women. I tried dating that type because at least they wouldn't want my money since they had their own, but they were so stuck-up that I couldn't even handle having a conversation with them, and it was even worse in bed— imagine a dead starfish lying in the center of the bed.

So, for now, I'm just cruising along, focusing on work and my future. I might be getting older, but I figure I still have plenty of time to find the right woman.

"So, I hear congratulations are in order," I say once we throw our bags onto the back of the golf cart and jump in—Samuel driving. "Retirement, huh?"

"Yeah." He chuckles. "That's actually what I wanted to talk to you about. I was hoping to speak to you before the article was published, but you were out of town on business, and I felt this conversation would be better in person."

My heart pounds against my chest, as I hope this conversation is going where I think it is. Having been the Chief Operating Officer for the past seven years, there's only one position higher than my current one—CEO. And since that position has been Samuel's and I thought it would remain his until the day he died, I never put it into my head there was a chance of me getting it. But now, with him formally stepping down, the position is open.

"A year ago, if anyone had said I'd be retiring at sixty, I would've laughed in their face," he says, driving over to the first hole. He parks, but doesn't attempt to get out, so I stay put as well. "This business has been my entire life since I started it almost forty years ago."

I nod in understanding, knowing firsthand how hard of a worker he is—or was, until he met his now wife. Lately, he's been spending more time with her than at the office.

"I've watched you grow up from a lost teenage boy to a hardworking businessman," he continues, turning to face me. "And I'm so proud of everything you've learned and accomplished."

I listen, waiting and hoping for the words to come.

"A year ago, you would've been my only choice for CEO, but I've been doing a lot of soul-searching the past several months, and I don't want whoever steps into my position to make the same mistakes I made. You remind me of myself when I was your age, and while that's a good thing businesswise, it's also a recipe for self-destruction."

I say nothing, confused as fuck and hoping he'll explain what the hell he's talking about.

"I want someone hardworking to become the new CEO, which you are," he adds. "But I also want someone who has and understands family values. After all, he or she is going to be the new face of the company. I'm not saying they have to be married, but I'm looking for someone who can take what I've created and make it more family friendly."

He scratches his neatly trimmed beard, looking off into the distance like he's thinking, so I stay quiet, figuring he's not done yet. And sure enough, he continues a moment later.

"Did you know that Rhonda in advertising quit after she had a baby? She wanted to be home with her baby and HR told her if she couldn't meet the forty-hour requirement, she would be let go. I want someone like Rhonda to feel like this company is her family."

I stare at Samuel, wondering if I'm being punked, but from his expression, I know he's serious.

"My daughter practically grew up in that office building, yet I barely know her," he says softly, his voice filled with unshed emotion. "I destroyed my family for this company, and I won't allow it to destroy anyone else. I need someone who can be not only the face of the company, but also back it up with their actions."

Jesus fucking Christ. Who is this guy, and what did he do with the man whose mantra used to be, *If you're not in the office before the sun rises and you leave before it sets, you're not working hard enough*?

He goes on, "I want company get-togethers, new maternity and paternity policies, and I'm not sure you're the right person to do that."

"Not the right person?" I choke out. As his COO, I'm already pretty much running the company, especially since he hasn't been around in months. "If you want these changes, I can implement them."

He sighs and shakes his head. "I know you're capable of running the company I've built from the ground up, but you're almost forty"—thirty-eight, but that's beside the point—"and you have no desire to start a family of your own. You work as many, if not more, hours than I ever did, and I get it, Julian. You've busted your ass to get to where you are, and I'm not trying to punish you for it.

"But not only does appointing a single man who has never settled down in his life look bad, but my fear is that someone like you taking over would mean the company would continue to run in the same manner. And worse"—he locks eyes with me—"I'm fearful that you becoming the CEO would mean history repeating itself, and the last thing I want is for you to miss out on love because of business.

"Now," he continues, "that's not to say you're not in the running. I won't be announcing the new CEO until the end of the year, so anything can happen. But I just wanted you to know where I stand. I'm hoping to hire from within, so I'll be making my short list and watching everything going on at work for the next several months before I make my decision." He pats me on my shoulder and grins. "All right, enough shoptalk. Let's go hit a few balls."

He hops out of the golf cart and grabs his bag like he didn't just light the match that blew up my entire world.

"So, let me get this straight," my best friend, Ryder, says. "He's not requiring the CEO to be married, but he's looking for a family man."

"Or woman."

"Or woman," he parrots. "I don't know. It sounds to me like now that he's married and all happy and in love, he wants the person who's going to take his position to have the same outlook on life."

"Exactly," I agree, throwing back my glass of scotch. "And how the fuck am I supposed to compete with that when I'm not even in a relationship?"

"You could meet someone."

"Yeah, because that's the perfect way to start a relationship."

"Well, you could always hire a wife." He grins and sips his drink.

"Hire an escort?" I hiss. "That's illegal, and I'm not about to risk jail time to be CEO. Besides, my luck, that shit would come out at the wrong time and explode in my face."

"Or you could contact one of those trophy-wife agencies. It's completely legal. Like Match for the wealthy."

"That's actually a thing?"

"Of course it is."

He pulls out his phone—no doubt to text his fiancée, who I'm sure knows exactly how to find a wealthy man. Nora Arnold comes from money, but not the kind Ryder has. It's enough to run in the same circles—hence how they met—but not enough for her to be rich in her own right.

Unlike my best friend, she doesn't have a trust fund worth millions of dollars, which means, in order for her to live the lifestyle she believes is owed to her, she'll have to marry a wealthy man.

Women like Nora were born and bred to marry rich. She went to college, majoring in some bullshit degree because that's what's expected, but she's never worked a day in her life, aside from "helping out" at her father's company, which stopped the second she convinced Ryder to let her move in with him.

But he says he cares about her, so I keep my mouth shut and hope she never screws him over.

While we wait for Nora to respond, I ask, "You're not going for the position?"

He's the CFO, so it wouldn't be unheard of for him to try for the CEO position.

"Nah," he says. "I like it right where I am. Nora would probably kill me if she knew I was giving up the opportunity for a promotion, but"—he shrugs—"she won't find out, so it's all good."

I bite back what I want to say and nod. Ryder is a damn good guy despite his partner of choice. We met several years back when he was hired in accounting and have been friends ever since. He doesn't care that I didn't graduate from some Ivy League university, like most other people. He still views and respects me as an equal.

His phone beeps with an incoming text, and he slides it over to me.

"Here you go," he says. "Trophy Wives R Us."

Three

ANASTASIA
THREE MONTHS LATER

I can't believe I'm doing this. I mean, I can believe it since I'm here, on US soil. But I can't believe it actually happened.

After the first month of radio silence, I started to get worried that my plan wasn't going to come to fruition. I knew the chances of a wealthy man looking for a trophy wife in the Houston area were slim, but I held out hope because Texas was one of the wealthiest states. But then, after almost two months of me sweating it out, I received the call.

Ian Thomas, age thirty-eight. Brown hair, green eyes, works as a COO for a Fortune 500 company, and is looking for a trophy wife.

We spent the next three weeks emailing and then eventually texting back and forth. He explained that he wasn't actually looking for marriage. He needed someone to be by his side for several upcoming events and wasn't interested in hiring an escort. He needed it to appear real and felt the best way for that to happen was for a woman to move in and play house.

I not only respect his honesty, but it makes me feel better since I have zero intention of marrying this guy, and once I prove to my dad that I can be the CEO he's looking for, all bets are off.

Because the service we used—and he paid for—would only match people who seemed to work together, the specifics were left to be handled between us. We agreed to a one-year fake engagement, and in exchange, at the end of the year, I would receive a whopping ten mil.

To most, that would be a lot of money, especially for only a year's worth of time, but I was raised with wealth, and my trust alone is in the high nine figures. So, his ten million is chump change, and if I can convince my dad to hire me as the CEO, I'm dropping this guy like a bad habit, and he can keep his money.

Of course, since I was pretending to be a ditsy gold digger, I didn't tell him that. Instead, I happily agreed … after insisting on a vehicle, a whole new wardrobe, and an allowance—you know, since I have to play the part.

And last week, he officially asked me to move to Texas. I was shocked to learn that he wasn't actually in Houston, but in Rosemary—the city I had been born and raised in. I was a little concerned about moving in with a strange man, but the service we used ran thorough background checks on both parties before allowing them to use their service.

Since I had already quit my job, I hired a realtor to rent out my flat and paid a shipping company to bring all my stuff to the States and store it in a local storage facility. If I get the position—which I can't imagine not getting—I'll be permanently relocating to Rosemary since Kingston's headquarters and distillery are here.

I step off the plane, and the Texas heat nearly takes my breath away, my body having grown used to the cooler temperatures in London. But since I plan to stay, it's something I'll have to get used to.

"Good morning, ma'am. Did you have a good flight?" a gentleman holding a sign with my name asks.

I flew private, so of course I had a good flight. And it was even better, knowing Ian was footing the bill for it.

"Fabulous," I say, using the same high-pitched voice I used the few times Ian and I spoke over the phone. After spending several weeks watching reruns of *The Real Housewives*, I'm confident that I can pull this off.

In my Burberry stilettos and matching wraparound dress that accentuates all of my best physical features, I saunter toward the awaiting town car, letting the driver grab my luggage. The drive from the airport isn't long, and I use the time to set up the phone I purchased before coming here, which has a US number.

As we drive through Rosemary, I can't help but stare out the window. So much of the city has changed while I was away, yet it still feels the same. When I ran after my mom's death, I always knew I'd have to come back eventually, but I wasn't prepared for the overwhelming sense of nostalgia I feel as we pass the Kingston building. I make a mental note to visit Mom's grave since I haven't been by since we laid her to rest. I've thought about going a million times, but that would mean going home, and it just hurt too much.

When the driver pulls up to the elaborate wrought iron fence and we wait for the gate to open, I take a moment to check out my surroundings—the place I'll be calling home for at least the next several months. The long driveway leads up to a two-story home with a three-car garage. For the area it's in, it's on the modest side, but it's still beautiful in its own right.

The driver pulls around, stopping in front of the large mahogany double doors, and I take a moment to reapply my blood-red lipstick.

I'm not a huge makeup person, but Mom always said, "Red lipstick is the weapon for savage women."

I'm not sure if she made up the quote or read it somewhere, but she always wore red lipstick, and in turn, so do I.

The driver rounds the car as I put my lipstick away and mentally psych myself up.

When he opens the door, taking my hand to help me out, I murmur, "Thank you," just as the front door opens and a gentleman, dressed to the nines in a power suit, steps out.

His dark brown hair is messy in that way that only men can get away with, and the scruff on his face is neatly trimmed. I saw a picture of him from the matchmaking service we used, but it didn't do him justice. It looked like a mug shot, whereas in person, he looks like a goddamn *GQ* model.

Ian takes a step forward, his hands resting casually in his pockets, as if he doesn't have a care in the world. As his gaze ascends my body, taking in every inch of me, I stand still, letting him check out what he's paid for, knowing that I'm a beautiful woman. I eat healthy, work out regularly, and have a naturally curvy body with ample cleavage that almost looks paid for, but isn't.

When he's done checking me out, his emerald eyes meet mine, and I suck in a sharp breath, overcome with a bout of lust I wasn't expecting to overtake my body.

Until this moment, I thought I knew what I was getting myself into. I figured I would play housewife in the morning and evenings, and while he was at work, I'd do my own thing. But what I didn't think about is the fact that I'm going to be living with a wealthy, powerful, gorgeous older man who expects me to meet his needs—and that includes sex.

Don't get me wrong. I'm no virgin. I have my own needs, and I'm no stranger to having them met. But usually, once the orgasms have subsided and we're both left sated, we go our separate ways. Except now, there's nowhere to go.

"Sir," the driver says, his voice cutting through the sexual fog. "Her bags."

"Thank you. That will be all." Ian nods once, and the driver scurries back into the car and takes off.

Leaving my bags for Ian to take, I square my shoulders, jut out my breasts, and saunter up to him, ready to play my part. I stop directly in front of him and lean in, placing my hands on his biceps and kissing his cheek. I let my lips linger just a tad too long, knowing I need to seduce this man if I'm going to convince him to play the part of my doting husband in front of my dad— I'll deal with him finding out I'm a businesswoman and not an actual trophy wife later. But it's a double-edged sword because during that time, I inhale his masculine scent. It's woodsy with a hint of spice that flows through my veins and straight to my lady parts, like a direct hit of dopamine.

Holy shit! How the hell can a man smell so sexy?

I stumble back, needing to clear my head, and Ian raises a brow. He's shrewd—noted.

"Stacey," he says smoothly, his voice deep and masculine as he speaks the nickname I gave on my résumé, not wanting to use my real name, "welcome home."

I swallow nervously at his choice of words. It's doubtful he meant anything by it since he's made it clear this is temporary, but the word triggers something deep inside of me. The last time I had a home was when my mom was alive. Since the moment she took her final breath, I've felt like I no longer have a home.

Images of family dinners and holidays flit through my brain, and I immediately push them aside. This isn't my home. It's a means to an end. A temporary dwelling, where I'll sleep and eat while showing my dad that I'm capable of doing what he couldn't do—run a company successfully without destroying everyone around him. Just because he made mistake after mistake doesn't mean I will.

Ian clears his throat, and I realize I haven't said anything in return, too lost in my thoughts.

"Thank you," I breathe. "Your home is lovely."

He tilts his head to the side, and I have no idea why he's looking at me in confusion until he says, "You sound different in person than on the phone."

It takes me a second to wrap my head around his words, but once I do, I curse myself to hell. I forgot to use my trophy-wife voice! Shit.

"I do?" I squeak out, playing dumb.

"It's a good thing," he says with a grin. "I like your voice better like this."

"Want to show me around?" I ask to change the subject.

"Of course," he says, walking around me to grab my bags.

When we enter his home, I stop in the foyer and take it all in. The color scheme is black, white, and gray. The living room is large with a ridiculously big flat-screen TV, plush black leather couches, and a wet bar that rivals a real bar. I don't have to see the rest of the house to know this is the quintessential bachelor pad.

"Do you have a pool table somewhere?" I ask, half joking.

He chuckles. "I do. In the billiards room." He shrugs. "I also have a pool, a hot tub, a gym, and a kick-ass outdoor grill." He leans in, and before I can hold my breath, I inhale another whiff of that damn scent. "When I'm not working, I enjoy having some of my close friends over to barbecue and watch a game. Do you enjoy watching sports?"

"I once dated a guy on the lacrosse team, and that was fun to watch," I blurt out. "But aside from that, I couldn't tell you anything about any sports." I cringe at my word vomit, but in my defense, the delicious smell of him is getting to my head and making me dizzy—and maybe stupid.

Ian barks out a melodic laugh as he steps around me. "Well, since you'll be living here for the next year, I'm sure I can teach you a thing or two about sports."

He shoots me a playful wink that goes straight to the apex of my legs, and I internally groan at the way this man is affecting me. I'm Anastasia Belle Kingston-Webb. I don't let men affect me.

Jesus, get it together, woman!

He shows me the rest of the downstairs, and despite it having a bachelor-pad vibe, it's tastefully done.

When we get upstairs, he stops at the first door on the left. "This is my room."

I peek inside, but don't walk in since he hasn't done so. It has the same color palette as the rest of the house, only unlike the rest of the house that looks barely lived in, his king-size bed is a bit messy, telling me he actually sleeps in here and made his bed himself.

"Since we don't really know each other well and our engagement isn't real, I figured you'd be more comfortable in one of the guest rooms," he says as he closes the door to his room and walks a little farther down the hall.

He opens the door on the other side of the hallway and steps in, rolling my luggage behind him. "This is your room. If you need or want anything changed, just let me know. It has an en suite bathroom with a Jacuzzi tub."

"Thank you," I murmur, checking the room out.

"I was thinking we could go to dinner tonight, and maybe tomorrow, if you're up for it, we could go on the boat."

"You don't have to work?"

"I, uh …" He clears his throat. "I took the weekend off so we could get to know each other … in person."

He smiles shyly, and my heart rate picks up speed.

"The truth is, I've never done anything like this before, and I had no idea what to expect. I wasn't even convinced you'd show up."

I laugh and nod in agreement. "I get it. I can't believe I actually got on the plane. The last time I did something this crazy was when I was in high school and begging for my dad's attention—" I snap my mouth closed and mentally smack myself for once again not being careful with what I say.

"Well, now, you can't leave me hanging," he says with a grin. "What was this crazy thing you did?"

"I, uh …" My cheeks warm at the thought before the words even make it out. "I got drunk at a charity function, and a bunch of my friends and I went skinny-dipping in the pool … that no one else was swimming in."

I cover my face with my hands, and Ian laughs.

"Damn, does that mean I can expect you to go skinny-dipping in my pool when you want my attention?"

I groan and shake my head. "Not happening," I mutter from under my hands.

"Well, a man can hope," he murmurs.

When I get the courage to look at him again, he's staring at me, his green eyes soft and curious.

"What?" I ask, wanting to know what he's thinking.

"I thought you were going to be this airhead trophy wife. No offense," he adds quickly. "But you're different."

"Different good or different bad?" I ask even though I shouldn't care one way or another. I'm using this guy as much as he's using me. Who cares how he sees me?

"Good," he says. "Definitely good."

It shouldn't, but the way he says those words, while looking at me with appreciation and approval, pleases me.

"I know you had a long flight, so I'll let you get situated, maybe take a nap. How about dinner at six?"

"That sounds perfect."

"If you need anything, please don't hesitate to ask," he says.

Then, he leans in and kisses my cheek. It's only a brush of his lips, so soft that they barely touch my flesh, but it's enough to send shivers of pleasure racing through my body and leave me wondering what the hell I've gotten myself into.

Once he's gone, instead of napping, I call my dad, wanting to get the ball rolling.

"Hello?" he says, not recognizing the number.

"Hey, Dad," I say back.

"Anastasia! Are you in town? That area code is local." The excitement in his tone causes a lump of emotion to clog my airway.

"Yeah," I choke out. "I am. Remember that guy I told you I was seeing?"

To help set the scene so it doesn't look as fake as it is, I've mentioned seeing a guy when we talked the past few times. I wasn't sure if this would actually happen, but I figured, worst-case scenario, I'd tell him we broke up. But since I'm here, I can move forward with my plan.

"I do," he says slowly.

"Well, I didn't want to say anything because I wasn't sure how serious we were, but he lives in Texas. In Rosemary actually."

"And you're visiting him?" Dad asks, no judgment in his tone.

"Actually, we're engaged ... and I moved here."

"Oh, sweetie, I'm so happy for you. What about your job in London?"

"I quit."

"Wow, he must mean a lot to you. What did you say his name is again?"

"Ian Thomas."

Dad thinks for a second, then says, "Doesn't ring any bells. So, any chance of seeing my daughter since she's in the same zip code and possibly meeting the man who's stolen her heart?"

"I'd like that," I say. "I'm not sure when, but this week, maybe you and I can do lunch."

"I would love that. Thank you."

We talk for a few more minutes and then hang up. As I set my phone down, instead of feeling the usual pain toward my dad, today, guilt settles inside my belly like a dead weight. I don't know if it's because I'm lying to him about falling in love or because I've been gone so long and he sounded genuinely happy to know I'm back while I have ulterior motives that he isn't aware of, but something deep inside me tells me that I need to proceed with caution before I make decisions I can't take back.

All of this started with my dad's choices that destroyed his family. The last thing I want is to, as he said, make the same mistakes he made.

Four

JUL(IAN)

"WELL, YOU'RE ALIVE, SO I'M ASSUMING SHE'S NOT A serial killer?" Ryder asks through the line.

It's been about an hour since I left Stacey in her room, and I can't get her off my mind. I came down to my home office to try to get some work done since dinner isn't for a few hours, but the only thing I can think about is her—brown hair with caramel highlights, the brightest hazel eyes I've ever seen, curves for goddamn days. Fuck, and those plump red lips that I can't help but imagine wrapped around my cock. Cliché maybe, but I'm still a red-blooded male with fantasies, and my newest one is of her marking me with those red fucking lips.

"If she is, I'm so distracted by how gorgeous she is that she'd probably get away with murdering me," I murmur, making Ryder chuckle.

"So, what's the plan?"

"Dinner tonight, taking the boat out tomorrow. Maybe we'll go to brunch at the country club on Sunday."

"Wow, look at you. You're like the welcoming committee."

"Shut up," I groan. "This is so weird. I've lived on my own for the past twenty years, and suddenly, I'm sharing my home with a gorgeous stranger, who's supposed to be my fiancée. I'm in over my head here."

"Breathe," Ryder says. "She knows the score and will be compensated well for it. Just take it one day at a time. Get to know her, and once you guys are comfortable around each other, introduce her to Samuel to get the ball rolling. Once he sees you're in a committed relationship, he'll have no choice but to take you into consideration for the CEO position. You were already his best candidate before he went soft."

"True," I agree, taking a deep breath.

"Hey, we should go on a double date," Ryder suggests, making me laugh. "I bet the women would hit it off."

I think back to the way Stacey presented herself. On the phone, she sounded a lot like Nora, Ryder's fiancée, and I was mentally prepared to have to deal with a woman like that for the next year. But then she got out of the car, and it was as if she was a completely different person. She was sweet and witty and not the least bit annoying, like I'd expected her to be. I laugh to myself, remembering her comment about skinny-dipping. I don't know why, but something is telling me there's more to her than what meets the eye.

"Yeah, maybe," I say noncommittally, needing to spend some time with Stacey to get a better grasp on the type of woman she is.

I could be wrong, but from our brief interaction today, she didn't come across like the typical *trophy wife*. But maybe she was just nervous, and her true personality will come out the more time we spend together.

I spend the next couple of hours getting a few things done and then head upstairs to shower and get dressed for dinner. I didn't tell Stacey where we were going or the dress code, so I'm about to walk across the hall to let her know that it's an upscale restaurant so she can dress accordingly, but then she steps out of the room.

Unlike earlier, where her hair was up in a loose ponytail, it's down and straight, framing her beautifully done-up face. She's donning a maroon dress that's short in the front and longer in the back, accentuating her creamy thighs. It dips low up top, showing off the swells of her breasts. And when my eyes land on her black stilettos with the red soles that match the color of her lips, my first thought is that I want to say fuck it to dinner and take her against the wall while she digs her heels into my back.

"I wasn't sure where we were going or how to dress," she says.

"You look perfect," I tell her, closing the gap between us. "I was going to wait until dinner to give you this, but I would love it if you wore it now."

I reach into my suit pocket and pull out a black box. "I know what's between us isn't real," I say, snapping the box open. "But while you're living here, I have every intention of treating you like I would my fiancée—with respect and loyalty."

I take the engagement ring out of the box that I picked out earlier this week. I wasn't sure what to go with since Nora has a huge rock on her finger, and I imagined most trophy wives would prefer something similar, but when I got to the store, I ended up going with something I would want my fiancée to wear. It's not big or flashy, but …

"It's beautiful," Stacey breathes as I take her delicate left hand in mine and slide the ring onto her finger. "I'll take good care of it." She admires the ring for several moments and then glances up at me. "I know this isn't real, but you can expect the same from me."

I nod. "Thank you."

Taking her arm in mine, I guide her down the stairs and out to the garage. Since this is Texas, I have two vehicles—a truck and a sports car. Tonight calls for the sports car.

"May I?" she asks when my phone connects to the Bluetooth and my playlist pops up.

"Sure."

She takes my phone and scrolls through the playlist, stopping on "Blank Space" by Taylor Swift, and clicks play.

"So, you're a Swiftie, huh?" she says with a laugh that goes straight to my cock.

"Nah." I shake my head. "That would be my little sister, Jessika. I swear she listened to this shit on repeat when it first came out."

"I did too," she admits, reminding me that she's a good ten years younger than me. "Are you guys close?"

"Yeah, we are. Despite the fourteen-year age difference and her being a pain in the ass most days, she's one of my best friends."

I notice in my peripheral vision that Stacey's eyes go wide. "Wow, that's a huge age gap."

"Mom had me at sixteen, and my sperm donor wanted nothing to do with us. So, for years, it was just the two of us. When I was twelve, she met my stepdad, Frank. They fell in love and got married, and a couple of years later, Jessika came along."

I smile to myself, remembering how much I loved her from the moment I met her. She was just this perfect little thing that wanted to be loved.

"Does your family live here too?" she asks.

"Yeah, Frank runs a luxury auto garage downtown called Prestige Auto, and my mom helps him run it. My sister is in law school."

Since my parents technically make too much for financial aid, but not enough to pay for her schooling, I pay for it, not wanting her to graduate with loans.

"That's awesome," Stacey says. "What kind of lawyer does she want to be?"

"Nonprofit," I groan. "She's all about volunteering and helping others. She wants to assist organizations who need it and people who need legal assistance but can't afford it."

"And I take it, you don't agree with that concentration?"

"Corporate law would be—"

"Boring as hell," she finishes. "Why would anyone who enjoys helping others want to be stuck in an office all day, drawing up contracts for million-dollar corporations that are demanding, selfish, and full of themselves? Arguing with megalomaniacs about the laws and regulations? The hours are long and stressful."

She shakes her head, and I take my eyes off the road to stare at her, shocked that she knows so much about corporate law. If I were having this conversation with Nora, the only point she'd be able to make was which one brought in more money.

When Stacey catches me looking at her, her cheeks turn a beautiful shade of pink, and she clears her throat. "Anyway, I think she should follow her passion."

She tries to play it off, but it's too late. I see her—the *real* her. This woman is a paradox, and I don't know what to make of it.

"Did you go to college?" I ask casually, noting the way she momentarily tenses up before relaxing. If I wasn't paying attention, I would've missed it, but something is off here, and I'm on high alert now.

I'm not concerned about the legalities of our agreement. Everything was done on the up-and-up. But something isn't adding up. Stacey hasn't been given a dime yet, but she's wearing designer clothes, telling me she has her own money. On top of that, she speaks properly and knows about law.

"I did," she says, answering my question without giving shit away.

"I'm assuming you didn't major in corporate law?" I joke.

She laughs, but it sounds off compared to her natural, light laugh I've heard several times already.

"No," she says, still refusing to give anything away.

I consider pushing the subject, but we arrive at 365—the restaurant we're eating dinner at—and need to get out so the valet can park the car. With her on my arm, I lead us inside, and we're shown to our table on the terrace.

The waiter introduces himself, lists the specials, and then asks what we would like to drink.

"I'll have a scotch, neat," I tell him. "Kingston Gold Label, if you have it."

The waiter nods, but Stacey looks at me like I've grown two heads, and I briefly wonder if she's not a drinker.

Until she clears her throat and plasters on a smile, barely glancing at the wine list before she says, "I'll have a glass of 2003 Marcassin pinot noir."

"We only serve that by the bottle," the waiter states.

"That's fine," she says just before she looks back down at the list, her eyes going wide. "Oh, um, actually …" Her gaze flits to me and then the waiter. "I'll have—"

"We'll take the bottle," I tell the waiter. "Thank you."

As a man who's worked for a liquor company half my life, I think what a person orders says a lot about them. I always order Kingston because I'm loyal to the company that's given me the life I live. This woman sitting in front of me just ordered a five-hundred-dollar bottle of wine. The price isn't what has my attention though. It's the fact that she knew what to order without thought. She not only knows her wines, but she also knows the good shit, and she didn't consider the price until it was brought to her attention.

She's either a seasoned gold digger, which doesn't fit the woman I've gotten to know thus far, or she's been around good alcohol. But here's the thing: why the hell would somebody apply to become a trophy wife for the pay, yet be accustomed to ordering expensive alcohol?

I could argue that she did it because I'm footing the bill, yet she ordered before she looked at the price, and once she realized how expensive it was, she backtracked.

There's a chance I'm overthinking this, but I didn't get to where I am without being scrupulous.

"You know your wines," I say once the waiter has retreated.

"I spent some time in Europe. It's pretty much a staple there," she says with a light laugh. "You can't eat out without learning which wines are better than others."

I remember that she's from Europe and mentally chastise myself. Of course she knows her wines. I'm being ridiculous, and if I'm honest, I think I might be looking for something to be off with her because so far, I can't find a single damn thing wrong with her. I was expecting a brainless bimbo, but instead got a smart, witty, beautiful woman.

I think a part of me is wondering why someone like her is here when she could easily land any man she wants. And that makes me wonder if maybe she's in some kind of trouble and she needs the payout. I want to ask, but it would sound accusatory, so instead, I push it aside. If something's wrong and she needs help, eventually, it will come out.

The waiter brings us our drinks of choice, and then we order our dinner. The rest of the meal goes well. We keep shit light, talking about places we've visited, our favorite hobbies and books and shows. She admits she hasn't been on a boat in years and is excited for tomorrow, and despite knowing this is all fake, I really enjoy her company. Stacey is easy to talk to, and if the circumstances were different, she's someone I would actually consider getting to know better—for real.

After dinner, I drive us home and walk her to her door. She doesn't open it though, instead turning around and facing me.

"Thank you for dinner," she says. "The food and wine were delicious, and the conversation was wonderful. It was probably one of the best fake dates I've been on in a long time."

Her eyes, filled with mirth, connect with mine, and I lean in to kiss her cheek good night.

My lips brush her soft skin, and I whisper against her ear, "I had a great night," before I back up, wishing the night weren't coming to an end.

As if she's having the same thought as me, she says, "So, tomorrow?"

"Be ready to go bright and early." I lean back in and kiss the corner of her mouth this time, before I retreat to my room, where I spend the next twenty minutes jacking off while I think about my new *fake* fiancée.

"You're spoiling me," Stacey moans as I rub sunscreen along her shoulders and back. "Keep it up, and I'm going to expect delicious, fancy dinners and day trips on your boat every weekend."

I chuckle, moving my way down to the backs of her thighs while trying like hell to keep my cock from getting hard. But it's hard to do when the sexy woman in front of me is dressed in a string bikini that could be used to floss my teeth.

"I'm glad you're having a good time."

I finish applying the sunscreen and then climb over her, kissing her neck before I hop up. But before I make it far, she turns over and grabs the edge of my shorts.

"Can you do my front, please?" She playfully bats her lashes. "I don't want to get it all over my hands."

I internally groan, knowing my restraint is running thin and if I have to apply sunscreen to her breasts, I just might snap. She's been like this all day since the moment we woke up—touching and flirting. Walking around in her tiny bikini. Thank God it's just the two of us on the boat, or I might've lost my shit with jealousy. And I'm not usually a jealous guy.

"If you want me to touch you, all you have to do is say so," I flirt back because my fiancée might be fake, but the way I want to fuck her in every goddamn hole is real.

She doesn't reply. Instead, she lies back and closes her eyes, waiting for me to massage the sunscreen onto her. I squirt some in my hands and then start with her arms, where it's safe, then work my way to her breasts. When I massage circles into the swells of her breasts that aren't covered by the tiny, thin material, she releases a soft moan that goes straight to my cock.

"Fuck, woman, you're killing me." I rub the lotion into her smooth, flat stomach and then finish with her thighs and calves. Once I'm done, I get up, needing a drink to cool down.

I'm standing in the kitchen, drinking a beer, when I hear footsteps coming down. I turn around and find Stacey standing in front of me.

"I'm thirsty," she murmurs, taking my beer from me and slowly, seductively bringing it to her lips. "Mmm," she moans after she takes a sip and hands it back to me. "That tastes good."

Without taking my eyes off her, I set the beer on the counter and then hook my arm around her torso, pulling her toward me.

"I want to taste *you*," I murmur once our faces are only inches apart.

"So, do it."

Leaning in, I start with a kiss to her cheek, my lips relishing in her creamy skin. I take a moment to inhale her scent, and even with the fragrance of lotion on her, her smell is still intoxicating. I trail kisses along her jawline and over to her pouty mouth, which is void of her red lipstick today. I brush my lips against hers, first the bottom, then the top, taking a moment to memorize how soft her lips are.

I'm prepared to end it there, but before I break the kiss, she parts her lips, welcoming me in, and I slide my tongue inside, coaxing hers, reveling in the sweet taste. A sexy little moan comes from her, and I deepen the kiss. She sighs into me, her arms wrapping around my neck, and I force myself to step back before I take her right here against the counter.

When I look down at her bee-stung lips that have formed the sexiest fucking pout, I take another step back, needing to distance myself before I do something I'm not sure I'll regret.

"I'm sorry," she says, misunderstanding.

"You have nothing to be sorry for. I kissed you."

"I told you to. And then I kissed you back."

"And if I didn't stop it, I'd be fucking you right now," I admit.

"I wouldn't be opposed," she states shyly.

"Is that what you want?" I ask, closing the distance I just put between us. I cup the side of her face and use my thumb to lift her chin to look at me. "Is that what you want?" I repeat. "For me to fuck you?"

"That's up to you," she murmurs. "You're in charge here, Ian, not me."

Her words are like ice-cold water being poured down my swim trunks. Is that why she's been flirting with me all day? Does she think that's what's expected of her? And is that what I want? To fuck someone who is doing it because they're being paid to do so?

The answer is no ... *hell no*. I want to fuck her because I'm attracted to her, because she's the first woman in ... well, forever that I'm wanting to get to know better, wanting to spend more time with. For the first time, I can see myself spending the night with a woman and not wanting to kick her out in the morning.

And I want her to *want* to fuck me. But with her words, I'm reminded that she isn't here for me. Our chemistry might be off the charts. Sure, we can hold a conversation easily, and fuck if being with her doesn't feel as natural as breathing, but at the end of the day, she's here for the paycheck. The ring on her finger wasn't put there out of love. It's a possession to seal the deal, to make it look legit.

Before she arrived, I thought about this, figured if neither one of us wanted to go a year without sex and she was down, I'd throw it out there that I was down to fuck. But what I didn't consider was that I would be so damn attracted to her that I wouldn't look at having sex with her as a chore.

And as I stare at this woman who has me feeling so much in such a short time, I wonder why the hell I couldn't have met her at a bar or a club and gotten to know her. Because then we'd both be here with the same goal in mind. But life doesn't work that way, and she's here for the money, which means if I fuck her right now, it's as if I'm paying her to do so.

But then an idea hits me. One I can't believe I'm even considering. What if we get to know each other and give this whole thing between us a real go? Fuck, the idea is crazy, borderline insane, but what if she's the one? Maybe my conversation with Samuel is getting to my head and making me soft. But it's something I need to figure out before we take things any further.

And so, instead of doing what my cock wants me to do—lift her by her ass and set her on the counter so

I can fuck her seven ways to Sunday—I think with my head and heart and take a step back.

"I want you," I tell her truthfully. "But I think we should take things slow."

"I don't understand," she says, her brows furrowing together in confusion. "Did I do something wrong?"

"No." I shake my head, feeling like I'm fucking this all up, which doesn't surprise me since I've never been in this situation before. "It's just that every woman in my life has always been nothing more than a one-night stand, and for the first time, I think I want something more with you."

Her eyes go as wide as saucers, and she jumps off the counter, putting distance between us. "More, as in wanting a fake fiancée, right?"

I'm not even sure what the hell she's asking, but the panic in her voice has me taking a step back. This is too soon. She's not there yet, which makes sense since we've only known each other for a fucking minute and I'm acting crazy.

I blame Samuel completely for this. Before our stupid talk, I was doing just fine. But then he had to go and point out how I'm getting older, and I haven't started a family yet. And how great it is to be in love and that he wants that for everyone. And now, here I am, losing my damn mind over the first woman I've been attracted to on a deeper level.

"Ian," Stacey says, "when you said you want more, you meant that you want me as your fake fiancée and not a one-night stand, right?"

This time, she words the question so I understand what she's asking and silently not saying—this can't be anything more than a fake engagement.

"Yeah," I choke out, backtracking. "I just meant that we should take things slow because we're going to be spending a lot of time together and we don't want to rush into shit. You know?"

"Yeah." She nods slowly. "That's what I thought you meant." She steps toward me and places her hand on my bicep. "But if you change your mind ... regarding sex, I'm here."

And with those parting words, she saunters away, leaving me wondering if there's something in my drink because if I didn't know better, I would think I'm drunk on this fucking woman. I've known her for two damn days, and I was ready to profess ... what, my love for her?

Thank God at least one of us is sober enough to think straight.

Five

ANASTASIA

THE PAST SEVENTY-TWO HOURS HAVE FELT LIKE SOME weird dream that I can't wake up from, and I'm not sure if I even want to. Ian Thomas has surprised me in more ways than one. He's not only sweet and romantic, but he's also gorgeous and nothing like I expected the businessman who was looking for a trophy wife to be like.

We've spent the weekend with him wining and dining me and showing me a good time while we get to know each other on a more personal level. I haven't taken this much time off from work in God knows how long, and it's been nice, enjoying some time relaxing and not having to worry about analyzing marketing data and consumer reports.

I came here with the goal of using Ian to get to my dad and his company and never thought in a million years that I would feel something *more*. So, when he told me he wanted to take things slow, I damn near lost my shit, thinking he was feeling something as well.

Thankfully, I misunderstood, and he just meant that he didn't want to jump into bed yet since this was all new. I meant what I said about not wanting to repeat my dad's mistakes, and the last thing I need is to start a new relationship while trying to convince my dad I'm the right person to run Kingston. All my attention needs to be on the company and my future.

Maybe if my dad had focused on the company instead of trying to have it all by marrying my mom and getting her pregnant, things wouldn't have gone down the way they did. Don't get me wrong. I'm thankful to be alive. But I didn't ask to be born, and after watching what my parents went through and wishing my dad would give me the attention I craved while I was growing up, I'd never be dumb enough to do things the way he did.

With that said, that doesn't mean I can't successfully run the company with the vision he has. I don't have to be married with kids to be a positive face of the company. That's just his bleeding heart talking.

After spending the rest of the day on the boat, Ian and I went to dinner and then spent the evening binge-watching movies neither of us had taken the time to watch.

On Sunday, he was supposed to take me to the country club, but instead, we spent the day by his pool, making out, swimming, and eating, enjoying the last day of our little bubble we'd created.

Now, it's Monday, and he left early this morning for work—which reminds me that I should probably ask him where he works. We were so focused on each other this weekend that we didn't get into details about anything in the outside world. And although I don't *need* to know details like that, I find myself *wanting* to know more about him.

But right now, my mind needs to be clear because I'm on my way to meet my dad for breakfast. I haven't seen him in six years—since my mom's funeral—and my feelings are all over the place.

I pull up to the restaurant we agreed to meet at and get out, handing the valet my keys. Ian got me a beautiful Mercedes crossover. He asked what kind of vehicle I wanted, and since I've barely driven since moving to London, I told him something safe, but not too big. He did good—that's for sure.

When I get to the hostess stand and give her my dad's name since he made the reservations, I'm taken back to a small, private room, where I find my dad waiting for me.

When our matching hazel eyes meet, I stop in my spot and suck in a harsh breath, seeing how much he's aged since the last time I saw him. His once-salt-and-pepper hair is now mostly all salt with only a little pepper. And the lines around his eyes have increased. He's lost a bit of weight, but he still looks like the man I remember. The man I looked up to and wanted to be just like.

His eyes turn glassy with emotion, and every negative feeling I had toward him is washed away with the tears that are sliding down his cheeks. Suddenly, the anger I felt just doesn't fucking matter. Nothing but being here with him does.

"Anastasia," he chokes out, standing and making his way toward me.

"Daddy."

He wraps his arms around me in the most comforting hug, and I inhale his signature scent. It's been six years since I've felt my dad's arms around me, since I smelled his signature scent—spicy, mixed with a hint of the cigars he's been smoking since before I was born—and I find myself getting choked up.

"I'm so sorry it took me so long to see you," I cry into his chest, hating that I went this long without seeing him.

He's the only parent I have left. I shouldn't have spent the last several years holding a grudge against him when I could have been enjoying his company. God, I was so stupid. What if something had happened to him while I was thousands of miles away, being stubborn?

"No, no apologies, my sweet girl," he coos, rubbing my back. "I'm just so happy you're here now." He backs up slightly, and his eyes home in on my red lips. He smiles softly, most likely remembering how much my mom loved her red lipstick. "You look so beautiful and so much like your mom."

"Thank you."

We sit at the table, and the waiter pours us each a glass of water, then Dad orders us a bottle of wine to share. When I lift my glass to take a sip of water, he eyes my engagement ring and smiles.

"Tell me about this man who stole your heart."

I swallow thickly, suddenly wishing that I hadn't lied to him, but it's too late now. I already agreed to be Ian's fake fiancée, and I can't go back on my word because of my guilt.

"Well, as I told you, his name is Ian, and he's in the business world, like us." Since I don't know where he works, I leave it at that. "He's sweet and romantic, and we have a good time together." *All true statements.*

"I want to meet him. And I can't wait for you to meet Selene."

"I'd like that. I just need to check with him because he's busy with work." *And I haven't told him that my family is here and that I'm using him the same way he's using me.*

"He should be putting you first." He frowns.

"Dad," I sigh. "You of all people should know what it's like."

"I do," he says with a shake of his head. "And look where it got me. I lost my wife and daughter. If this man is smart, he won't make the same mistakes I made. No job should ever be more important than family."

"I know," I agree.

"Speaking of jobs," he says, "what are you doing for work now that you're back?"

"I'm not sure yet," I say because I wasn't planning to ask him to let me come to work for him yet. I want today to be about us. And I figure, over the next couple of weeks, I'll put out feelers and see where he stands. "I'm just taking things one day at a time."

Dad nods thoughtfully.

The waiter delivers the wine and pours us each a glass. We both approve, so he takes our order and then retreats.

"I've been thinking," Dad says once we're alone again. "How would you feel about coming to work for me? My marketing team has a spot available."

"I thought you said you didn't want to mix business with family."

"I don't," he sighs. "But you're my daughter, and I love you, and if you want to come work for Kingston, you deserve to. Plus, I would love to have you working in the same building as me."

"But not as your CEO," I mutter, hating that he doesn't believe in me.

"Why don't we take things slow?" he suggests. "Who knows? Maybe you'll spend a week working for Kingston and change your mind about wanting the CEO position."

"I won't," I assure him. "When do I start?"

"You don't need to discuss it with your fiancé first?" He nods toward my ring. "I know how badly you want to be considered for this position, but this type of job can put a strain on a relationship, especially a new one." He frowns. "Maybe this isn't a good idea. You've never been in a relationship before."

"I can handle being in a relationship and running a company," I assure him, pushing aside the guilt niggling at me for lying to my dad about my fake relationship.

But in my defense, he pushed me to this by refusing to see that a single woman was capable of being the face of a liquor company. Honestly, he's only doing this because he's fallen in love and wants everyone to feel what he's feeling. He's thinking with his heart instead of his brain.

"Okay," he concedes. "But on one condition. I don't want business to come between us. I've waited a long time to get you back, and I don't want to lose you again. I have a couple other people I'm considering for the position, and if you don't get it …"

"I'll understand," I tell him, knowing damn well I'm going to outshine every one of those other prospects.

Our meals are brought to the table, and we spend the rest of lunch catching up. I try to ask him about the company, but he refuses to discuss it, telling me that I can come in tomorrow and he'll show me around and have HR get me formally hired so I'm on the payroll.

"Speak to your fiancé and let me know when we can meet for dinner," Dad says while we wait for our cars at valet. "I can't wait to meet my future son-in-law."

"I will," I tell him, giving him a side hug, happy that I came home. Even if I don't get the position, coming back here was long overdue.

"Where are you going now?" Dad asks when our cars pull up.

"Actually ..." I clear my throat. "I was going to go visit Mom. I haven't been to her grave since we buried her."

"Would you like some company?" he offers, surprising me since he mentioned having a business meeting this afternoon.

"I thought you had to go to work."

He lifts my chin and meets my gaze. "I meant what I said, sweetie. Family first. If you want me there, I would love to join you. That meeting can be rescheduled."

"Thank you," I choke out, overcome with emotion. "I'd like that."

Six

ANASTASIA

IAN

I hope you're having a good day. My lunch meeting got moved to dinner. Can you please be ready to go at 6:00? It's at the country club. I'll be home early.

I GLANCE AT THE MESSAGE AS I WALK INTO THE HOUSE, sniffling back my tears. It was sent earlier, but I didn't look at it until now. The last thing I want to do is go to a business dinner tonight after spending the afternoon with my dad at the cemetery, but I have to uphold my end of the deal, so I need to get my shit together and leave the mourning to later.

"What happened?" Ian asks, making me jump.

I didn't park in the garage, so I wasn't aware he was already home.

"Nothing," I say, wiping my tears and forcing a fake smile.

"Don't lie to me." He closes the gap between us and pulls me into his arms, glancing down at me with concern etched on his features. "It's clear something is wrong, and I can't help if I don't know what it is."

My heart stutters in my chest. I'm not used to other people caring. It's not that no one cares, but I normally don't let anyone see me like this. Even at the gravesite with my dad, I didn't cry. It wasn't until after we left and I was alone in my car that I allowed myself to let go.

"I just came from visiting my mom's grave," I admit, shocking myself for letting Ian in so easily. "It's the first time I've been there since she passed away."

Ian envelops me in a comforting hug, and I allow myself to cry all over again.

"I knew it would be hard to see her grave," I tell him through my sobs. "But I didn't think it would feel like my heart was being ripped out of my chest all over again."

"You should've told me," he murmurs. "I would've come with you."

"I appreciate that, but my dad actually went with me."

"Your dad lives here?"

"Yeah, I grew up here." Speaking of which … "He saw my ring, so I had to tell him about you." Not exactly the truth, but not quite a lie either.

Ian's eyes go wide. "You told him?"

"That you're my fiancé? Yes."

I had to sign an NDA, agreeing not to tell anyone that our relationship was a lie, so it makes sense that I would tell my family and friends that I'm engaged. He just doesn't know that instead of telling my dad for Ian's benefit, I have my own agenda that happens to line up with his.

"How did he take it?"

"He wants to meet you."

Ian chuckles. "I've never met the parents before."

"My mom would've liked you," I say with a small laugh. "She would've thought you were ridiculously handsome and asked a million inappropriate questions."

The thought of my mom not being here to ever meet the man I choose to be with—if that day ever comes—has me feeling sad all over again.

Ian must pick up on my emotions because he says, "If you're not up for going to dinner tonight, I can cancel."

"No, I'm okay. It's not for a few hours, so that'll give me time to get myself together."

"Come with me."

He takes my hand in his and guides me upstairs, through my bedroom and into the bathroom. Ian lets go of my hand and turns the water on, then pours liquid in that immediately creates bubbles. The flow is strong and the tub is already halfway filled by the time Ian has lit a couple of candles and set them around the edge.

"While I go downstairs and get you a glass of wine to help you relax, get in and get comfortable." He presses a quick kiss to my lips and then disappears.

In a state of shock and awe, I undress and then climb into the tub, sighing as the heated water instantly calms me. Since the water is high enough and the bubbles are thick enough to cover the important parts, I switch the tap off and lean back, closing my eyes.

"Knock, knock," he says a few minutes later.

"You can come in."

He strides in and sets the glass of white wine on the edge, then walks over to the wall and presses a button that makes the jets in the tub turn on, hitting my back like the best massage.

"Better?" he asks.

"This is perfect," I choke out. "Thank you."

I can't remember the last time—if ever—someone took care of me like this. Not since my mom died and never like this.

Ian leans over and kisses me again, this time softer than the last, and butterflies flutter in my belly. As our lips curve around each other, I wonder if Ian was right about taking things slow because with every kiss and touch, it feels like we're toeing the imaginary line we drew, and if I'm not careful, he might just cross on over to my side. And I've yet to figure out if that's a good or bad thing.

"Close your eyes and relax," Ian murmurs, his lips brushing against mine once more. "If you need anything, let me know."

He stands, ready to give me time to myself, but before he can leave, I grab his bicep, halting him in place.

"This whole thing between us ... it's strictly physical, right?"

He looks at me for several seconds before he nods once. "Of course. Get some rest."

"Okay, good," I say. "Just making sure we're on the same page."

"*Definitely* on the same page," he agrees.

But as he walks out the door, I can't help but feel like although we're on the same page, we both might be in denial of the book we're reading.

THE RIDE TO THE COUNTRY CLUB IS QUIET. AND NOT the comfortable kind of quiet. It's awkward, and I hate it.

And since I'm not one to beat around the bush, when we pull up to the country club, before Ian can get out, I stop him and ask, "Did I do something wrong?"

"No," he says too quickly.

"Really? Because you were all over me, and then the moment I clarified our relationship was strictly physical, you got all weird."

Ian sighs. "Truth?"

"Always."

"I've never felt a connection with a woman the way I do with you," he says, palming the side of my face. "And when I mentioned wanting to take things slow, it was because I'd like to see where things go with us *for real*. But you've made it clear twice that's not what you're looking for, so ..." He shrugs. "I just need a moment to get my head on straight. But it's not your fault I caught

feelings for the only damn woman who isn't available."
He chuckles softly.

I consider telling him that it's not one-sided so he doesn't think he's the only one who has felt the connection, but before I can get the words out, a valet attendant steps up to my door and opens it.

"Can we continue this conversation after dinner?" I ask, hoping it will help make things less uncomfortable.

He went through all this trouble to have a fake fiancée on his arm, and I don't want our personal issues to affect his work engagement.

"Of course," he says, leaning over and kissing my cheek. "And in case I forgot to tell you, you look beautiful tonight."

With my arm linked in his, we walk up to the hostess stand.

"Kingston," Ian says, causing me to do a double take because did he just say …

No, I have to be hearing things, right?

"Yes, sir," she replies. "Mr. and Mrs. Kingston are already here. I'll show you back."

I'm so shocked by their conversation that I nearly trip over my heels and Ian has to save me.

"Are you okay?" he asks, continuing to follow the hostess back.

"Who is—"

Before I can finish my question, a masculine voice calls out my name. And not *Stacey*, the name Ian thinks is my real name. No, he says *Anastasia*. My real name.

"Dad," I whisper, my eyes meeting his.

"Dad?" Ian unhooks his arm from mine and takes a step back. "Wait, *Anastasia*?"

"Julian, what's going on here?" Dad asks, looking at my fake fiancé.

"Who's Julian?" I ask. "You mean Ian?"

But the second I say the names, my entire world turns on its axis because there's only one Julian that I know of …

"This sounds like a rendition of 'Who's on First?'" a woman says with a giggle.

I quickly glance at her and notice she's standing next to my dad. I recognize her from their wedding announcement. She's Selene, my dad's wife—my stepmom.

But I don't have time to focus on her because I'm too busy mentally kicking myself in the ass for not doing proper research. I mean, I looked up the key players at Kingston, I know the names of the COO and CFO, as well as several other employees, but I was so busy tying up loose ends at Benson that I didn't bother to look up pictures and details.

I told myself I would delve deeper once I was here and knew exactly who I was dealing with. I mean, the company has hundreds of employees working at Kingston's headquarters. It would've been a waste of time to look up people who weren't relevant. But that was dumb on my part because look where it's landed me—fake engaged to Julian Parker, the COO of Kingston Limited.

"Samuel is your dad?" Ian—err, Julian—questions.

"Yes," I snap, ready to go off on him until I glance at my dad, who's looking at us in confusion because he knows I'm engaged, yet I'm arguing with my fiancé over our names. "And this is your boss, right?" I say with a fake smile, trying to cover my tracks before my story is blown to pieces.

Julian glances at my dad. "I thought your daughter's name was Anastasia," he says, stating the obvious, but not connecting the dots yet.

"It is," I answer for my dad.

A look passes between Julian and me as he realizes that we're both guilty of the same thing—lying about our real names.

"Wait a second," Dad says, looking at Julian. "Is this your fiancée?" Then, to me, he adds, "You're engaged to my COO?"

"Did you two not discuss the important things, like family and work?" Selene pipes in, looking at us in bewilderment.

"We did. Just not the specifics," Julian says, pulling me into his side as I connect my own dots.

Julian wanted a trophy wife for the same reason I wanted a fake fiancé—to show my dad that he's a family man because just like me, Julian Parker is trying to become the next CEO of Kingston Limited—which means … I'm officially fake engaged to my enemy.

"To be honest," I lie, "we've been so caught up in each other that we didn't discuss things like that. I knew he was a COO, but I didn't know he worked for you." I glance up at Julian, trying like hell to look like I'm in love before I look back at my dad. "We've been totally lost in each other, in our own little bubble."

"So, this engagement is real?" Dad asks, sharp as always.

"Of course it is," I tell him, laying my head against Julian's chest to emphasize my claim. "I'm in love with this man, and I can't wait to marry him."

Dad nods slowly, his gaze flitting between the two of us, and I hold my breath, waiting for him to call us out on our shit. But then his face spreads into a smile, and the corners of his eyes crinkle with happiness.

"Well, all right then," he says, glancing at Julian. "Congratulations, son! I guess I have you to thank for bringing my daughter home."

He opens his arms, and Julian releases me to give my dad a hug.

When they separate, Dad looks at us both and chuckles. "Since you guys haven't discussed work, I'm assuming you haven't told Julian about what we talked about today."

"I haven't had time," I say, shaking my head.

"Work?" Julian raises a brow. "I thought you wanted to be a stay-at-home wife."

My dad barks out a laugh. "My daughter, a stay-at-home wife? That's funny. Are you going to tell him, or should I?"

"Tell me what?" Julian asks, his eyes staying trained on my dad.

When I don't say anything, Dad chuckles. "I hired Anastasia to work for me as a marketing analyst. She wants a chance to prove she can be the next face of Kingston. Your fiancée is your biggest competition to become the next CEO."

Julian slowly turns toward me. "Is that so?" he says with a devilish smirk that sends a shiver racing up my spine. "Well, soon-to-be *wifey*, it looks like we have a lot to discuss, don't we?"

Seven

SAMUEL KINGSTON

Julian and Anastasia must think falling in love has turned me blind, deaf, and dumb. But I can see past the way they're currently glaring at one another, hear the words they're not speaking, and despite the fact that they're not actually engaged—even though they want me to believe they are—I can feel the chemistry coming off them in waves. I could call them out on their lies, but I won't because for the first time since my late wife passed away, I have my daughter in the same zip code as me, and I can see what they can't—they're already falling in love.

I was afraid to let either of them take over as CEO, not because they aren't capable, but because they're both similar to me, and I love them too much to step down and watch either of them make the same mistakes I made. I'm not going to lie. I planned to give Julian the CEO position, but I was hoping by telling him that I didn't want to hire someone single, who would get absorbed in the company the same way I did, he would think about finally settling down. Selene warned me that manipulating people was wrong, but I was hoping that by putting the bug in his ear, he'd give it some thought.

But what I wasn't expecting was for my daughter to want to take over as CEO. And at first, that scared me because the last thing I want is for Anastasia to follow in my footsteps. It's something her mother never wanted for her, and when she died, I felt I owed it to her to honor her wishes.

Anastasia was raised in a home where her father put business before everything, and I think she's afraid to fall in love. Afraid to end up like her mother. She knows how the business world works. But love? That scares the shit out of her.

I wasn't sure what I was going to do when she got here, and then I realized I would have to choose between my daughter and the man who had become like a son to me. But now, I have a feeling they'll make the choice for me.

And if things go the way I hope, they'll choose love.

Eight

JULIAN

As everyone talks over dinner, I remain quiet for the most part, only adding to the conversation when a question is directed at me. Too much is going through my head. Stacey Webb—aka Anastasia Kingston-Webb, the woman I'm supposed to be paying ten million dollars to be my fake fiancée for the next year—is not only competing with me for the CEO position, but she's also worth hundreds of millions, which means she's been playing me from the beginning.

I have to give her credit though. What she did— attempting to play the willing trophy wife—was cunning. She needed a man on her arm because I'm sure her father gave her the same speech he gave me, so what does she do? She gets the *man* to pay for *her*, so she can claim she's engaged to be married.

I glance over at her, unsure if I should be pissed or in awe at how damn smart she is. I knew this though. The moment she stepped out of the town car and started to speak and when she was talking about my sister's major, I knew there was more to this woman than a gold digger trying to make some easy money by playing the doting fiancée.

Her father's talked about her over the years. She went to a private college and majored in business marketing, then went on to get her MBA in hospitality. Her dad would brag about how proud he was of her, and he even has a damn picture of her on his desk. She's in her cap and gown, but I never paid close attention to it. I guess I should've though because I literally invited my biggest competition into my home.

Well, you know what they say: *Keep your friends close and your enemies closer*. So, that's what I'm about to do because there's no way I'm going to give up my chance at becoming the next CEO. Anastasia might be his daughter, but I've given this company *everything* for the past twenty years, and I'll be damned if that woman comes off the bench and tries to take over the game.

"Have you guys discussed wedding dates or venues yet?" Selene asks, drawing me out of my thoughts.

Anastasia's hazel eyes, hidden under her thick lashes, meet mine, and her plump lips purse in annoyance before she looks back at her stepmom and plasters on a fake smile.

"We're just taking it one day at a time," she says. "With me about to start at Kingston and my dad retiring at the end of the year, I imagine we'll be so busy with work that it'll be a long engagement."

Samuel's brows furrow, and I know immediately the mistake Anastasia made before she does.

"It's not because of work," I add. "We just don't want to add more stuff to everyone's plate. It must be stressful, having to find a new CEO while planning your retirement."

Everything out of my mouth is bullshit since we didn't even know we were connected by her dad, but thankfully, Samuel nods, seeming to buy it.

"Please don't pick your wedding date based on my retirement," Samuel says. "I know firsthand what it's like to be in love and to not want to wait to get married."

He takes Selene's hand in his and brings it up to his mouth for a kiss. I'm used to their PDA, so it doesn't faze me, but I notice Anastasia suddenly looks uncomfortable, glancing around anywhere but at them.

"I think I'm going to call it a night," she says, setting her napkin on the table and standing abruptly. "I'm tired, and I'd like to get myself situated for tomorrow."

"Of course," her dad says.

Since he has an account here, we don't have to wait for the waiter to bring the bill, so we all stand as well and follow Anastasia out.

When our vehicles are brought around, we say a quick goodbye, and then Anastasia and I get into my car. She's quiet, and I could be wrong, but I don't think it's because of what went down between us.

I should probably mind my own business, but instead, I ask, "You okay?"

She flits her gaze toward me before she settles on staring out her window. "It's just hard," she whispers after a few beats. "He's like a different man with her, and I can't help but wonder why he couldn't be like that with my mom."

I nod in understanding. "I met your mom a few times," I say, unsure why I feel the need to tell her this story, but I guess I'm hoping it will help in some way. "She was really sweet. I had just started working for your dad, and I was in over my head. She bought me lunch, and while we ate, she told me everything I needed to know about your dad to ensure he wouldn't fire me. His likes, dislikes. Secrets nobody else would know."

Anastasia blows out a harsh breath, and I can see through the reflection in the window that her eyes are glassy.

"She said the reason why he saw something in me was because he used to be me—broke, lost, and just trying to find his place in this world," I continue. "She brought him lunch that day, too, but he was too busy to eat with her. She played it off like she didn't care, like she was used to it. But every Wednesday, she came to the office and brought him lunch, and every week, he told her he was too busy. Eventually, she stopped coming."

"When I was little, they used to have lunch every Wednesday. Dad used to say that he loved having lunch with us on Wednesdays because it helped him get through the rest of the week," she chokes out.

I stop at a light and look at Anastasia. "When she passed away, every Wednesday for probably two years, maybe longer, he sat at the conference table by himself. When I joined him one day, he said, 'If I could do one thing over again, it would be to have lunch with my wife on Wednesday one more time.'"

The tears spill over Anastasia's lids, but before they slide down her cheeks, she looks away. The light turns green, and the rest of our drive is quiet until we pull into the garage.

"My mom loved him with everything she had, and he broke her heart over and over again. I'm sure he has a lot of regrets. But it doesn't matter because she's gone and we can't rewind time."

"That's true. So, if you blame the company for everything, why is it so important for you to work there? I'd think it would be the last place you'd want to work."

Anastasia chuckles humorlessly. "I should probably hate Kingston Limited because he always chose it over us, but instead, I find myself wanting to be a part of it because of that very same reason. I grew up there. My dad would let me sit in on meetings, and I learned of my love for numbers there. Every night when he would get home, he would continue to work in his office, and I would hang out with him. He would explain it all to me and promise that, one day, I would work alongside him.

"But then I became a surly teenager, and his absence made me lash out, wanting nothing to do with Kingston. I got into the college of my choice, but I damn near failed out my freshman year. If it wasn't for my mom temporarily moving down there and reining me in, I probably would've failed out," she admits.

"She told me that the business owned him and if I wanted a relationship with him, I'd need to be a part of that world. She begged me to let my dream of working for Kingston go, but I couldn't do it.

"So, for the next few years, I busted my ass in school so I could go to work for him when I graduated." She sighs and shakes her head. "But then Mom was killed by that drunk driver, and I blamed my dad and ran away, not wanting anything to do with him or the company he'd chosen over us."

"And yet here you are, wanting to work for Kingston," I say, trying to understand.

"You know how I found out he was stepping down?" she asks. "From a friend who had read it online. I'm his daughter, his only blood relative left, and he didn't even offer me the position, knowing I'd been studying and working in this industry for most of my life. And when I called, upset, he told me he didn't feel I was the right person for the position."

"He said the same thing to me."

"But you aren't his child. You didn't sit with him every night, begging for his attention and hoping you would finally have it one day when you were running the family company together.

"To be honest, when I called him, I didn't even think I wanted the position, but then he told me I wasn't right for it, and something inside of me just ... broke." Her hazel eyes meet mine. "I shouldn't want or need his approval, but I do. I, Anastasia Belle Kingston-Webb, want my dad's approval. I want to prove to him I'm worthy of working for the company that means the most to him. The company he chose over his daughter and wife, the company he lived and breathed for my entire life."

She chokes out a sob, and I wish we weren't in the car so I could pull her into my arms and hold her. She cries for a few minutes and then takes a deep breath and lifts her head up, squaring her shoulders and looking into my eyes.

"I understand you've worked for Kingston for a long time, and you probably, in a lot of ways, deserve this position," she says, "but this is personal for me. I've never felt like I was enough for that man, but I'm going to show him that not only am I capable of running Kingston, but I'm also worthy of doing so."

I open my mouth, unsure of what I'm going to say, but before I can get a word out, she stops me.

"And before you point out my daddy issues, I'm already aware, and I accept them. My dad has gone soft, and he wants me to get married and pop out a couple of kids so I can do shit differently than he did.

"He wants a relationship with me, and he doesn't want to mix business and family, but what he doesn't get is that I might be like him in a lot of ways, but we differ in one big way. I'm not selfish enough to get married and have kids, knowing my work is my life. He destroyed his family because he wanted it all, but I know better."

Fuck, this woman. I can see the pain in her eyes, her desperation to prove herself to her father. And I can't even say I get it because my stepdad and I have a close relationship and I have no desire to have any type of relationship with my sperm donor. But what she doesn't understand is that I can't just walk away from this, which leaves us at an impasse.

"So, what do we do?" I ask, making it clear that I'm not backing down from the position.

When she realizes my intention behind my words, Anastasia's eyes turn into thin slits, going from emotional to savage in the blink of an eye. The transition is almost scary. "Once he knows you're not actually the family man you're pretending to be, he's not going to hire you," she says low, thinking she's got this all figured out.

I bark out a laugh. "Wow, look at you ... going from sweet to deadly in point-five seconds. By doing that, you'd be shooting yourself in the foot."

"Okay, then what do you suggest we do? Keep going with this ridiculous fake engagement?" She scoffs, like she can't even fathom being fake engaged to me when not too long ago, we were flirting and damn close to fucking.

"Actually, that's exactly what I propose we do. We continue this charade until he hires one of us to take his place."

She laughs. "You really think he's going to pick you over his own daughter?"

"Well, I think I have a damn good chance since he didn't ask you in the first place." It's a low blow, but, fuck, she's making it hard to be nice to her.

"Fuck you!" she spits, swinging open the car door and getting out.

"Don't be mad because I'm speaking the truth!" I call out, stalking after her.

When we get inside, she goes straight to the kitchen and grabs the bottle of wine from earlier, pouring herself a glass.

"You can talk all the shit you want," she says, taking a sip of the wine. "But you don't know me, and there's a reason why my dad says I'm just like him. When I want something, nothing and nobody will stop me from getting it."

"Okay, Red," I say, bridging the gap between us. "Challenge accepted."

I extend my hand, and she rolls her eyes.

"Red? Real original."

She clasps my hand, and we shake.

"May the best man—" I begin.

"Or woman," she corrects.

"May the best man *or woman* win," I say. And then with a smirk that I know will piss her off, I add, "Oh, and, Anastasia?"

She glares my way.

"I didn't nickname you Red because of your lips."

She raises a questioning brow. "Okay, so enlighten me."

"The red widow spider is one of the most beautiful yet deadly spiders. Just like you—beautiful but filled with venom. The only difference is, at this point, I probably know your father better than you do, so I know what you're capable of, and I won't be dumb enough to let you lure me in and bite me. I see you, Red, and when I stomp on your venomous ass, you're going to wish you'd stayed in London."

Nine

ANASTASIA

"Good morning. My name is—"

"Anastasia! It's a pleasure to meet you," the woman behind the desk says in a tone that's way too perky for nine in the morning. "My name is Josie. I'm your dad's and Julian's assistant."

She extends her hand, and I shake it, taking her in. She looks to be in her late thirties, maybe early forties. She's dressed professionally with cute, thick, black-framed glasses perched on her nose. I check out her left hand and notice she doesn't have a ring on her fourth finger.

"Nice to meet you," I tell her, mentally noting that I need to be careful with what I do and say around her.

She might work for my dad and Julian, but everyone knows the COO actually runs the show, which means she really works for Julian, and as we established last night when the line was redrawn, he's the enemy. She looks nice enough, but looks can be deceiving—Julian is the perfect example of that.

I'm not supposed to meet my dad until nine thirty for him to show me around, but I left early, needing to get out of that icy house. Julian was sitting at the table, drinking his coffee and scrolling on his phone, making it a point to ignore me. He hasn't said a word to me since he compared me to a venomous spider and threatened to stomp on me.

On the way to work, I stopped at the coffee shop across the street and enjoyed a latte and a muffin and then walked over here, hoping to check things out on my own before my dad arrived. Security got me set up with an employee ID and badge, and then I was taken to HR, who had me sign a million papers before welcoming me to Kingston Limited.

"Your dad should be in at any moment. If you want to have a seat in his office, you can head back." She points down the hall. "His door is on the left."

"Thank you," I tell her.

I'm heading toward his office when my phone pings with a text. I glance down at it to make sure it's not my dad, telling me he's running late, when I run into a wall. Well, not actually a wall. More like the very hard chest of my fake fiancé.

"I know you think the world revolves around you, but maybe you could watch where you're walking," he says, his glare cold enough to prevent those ice caps in Antarctica from melting.

"Maybe you ran into me," I volley.

"Except I was standing in the doorway, unmoving," he says dryly.

"Well, why would you do that?"

"Because I heard you out there and I figured I should probably join you since we're engaged and in love," he says, sarcasm dripping with each word. "C'mon. I'll show you around."

He engulfs my hand with his, and warmth spreads through me, thawing the ice and making me worried once again for global warming. The man shouldn't have this effect on my body, especially since I know he'd probably stand by and watch me choke to death without lifting a finger to help me, but my body has felt his warmth, my lips have tasted him, his scent is already ingrained in my brain, and it's so damn hard to separate what my body *feels* and what my brain *knows*.

"Your dad never gets here on time," he says as he guides me down the hall. "Selene makes him breakfast every morning, and he strolls in around ten."

It's so crazy to think about my dad *strolling in*, let alone so late. He always woke up before the sun came up and worked until late every night. Mom would have to practically pry him away from his desk just to have dinner with us.

We step into a room that I recognize from when I was younger, only it's been painted and updated.

"This is the break room." He points at each item. "Fridge, espresso machine, tables to eat at it if you don't want to eat in your office."

"I used to eat in here when I was younger, when the conference rooms were being used."

Memories of my mom packing me my lunch surface, but I push them back, not wanting to get emotional in front of Julian. The last thing I need is to show him any weakness.

"That's right. I forgot you grew up here." He glances at me.

"Yeah, we probably ran into each other and didn't know it."

"Not unless you were chilling in the mailroom. I was down there for four years, then an errand boy for another three …"

His implication of me starting damn near at the top doesn't go unnoticed, but I ignore it because I might be new to this company, but I've worked hard, and had I applied here without being blood related to the owner, I would've gotten the position I'm in with ease.

"When did you start working for my dad?"

"He took me under his wing when I was twenty-five."

"I stopped coming here when I was fourteen." With our ten-year age difference, it makes sense I never met him.

"I remember," he says. "Your dad wanted you to intern here, but you refused."

"Yeah, by then, I resented his job for taking all his time."

"Which is something I'll always regret," my dad says, making me spin around. "I hate that I didn't see what I was doing to my family, that I refused to listen. I thought I could buy your love, and I learned the hard way that it's not possible."

I swallow down the lump of emotion clogging my airway and nod, incapable of saying anything. Because of my refusal to speak to him for years and then keeping him at arm's length, he's never apologized—he's never been given the *chance* to apologize.

"I know you don't understand why I'm so hell-bent on the way I would like the direction of the company to go, but it's because of my mistakes. I don't want what happened to me to happen to either of you."

He glances from me to Julian, and it's then, in the way he looks at him, that I see how much my dad cares for Julian. He's not just his COO. He's like a son to him.

"That's not going to happen," Julian says, his eyes locked on my dad's. "I've been running the company successfully for the past seven years, and I have no problem implementing the changes you'd like."

"I actually have some great ideas," I add. "I've been doing research on corporate childcare, and I'd like to pitch my proposal to you once it's finalized."

Dad smiles. "That would be great, which leads me to my thoughts regarding both of you wanting to take over as CEO. After having conversations with a few other employees I was considering and them either not interested or not up for the task, it's down to you two." He darts his gaze between us. "Are you sure you're okay with going up against one another for the position? Your relationship is new and—"

"We're sure," I say despite the fact that Julian and I have barely spoken ten words to each other and none of them were regarding what would happen when *I* got the CEO position. "We've spoken at length and agreed there will be no hard feelings toward whoever gets it." I thread my fingers through Julian's to emphasize my point.

"And if you aren't selected," Dad says to me, "would you still like to work for Kingston?"

I never considered not getting the position, but now that he's mentioning it, my first thought is yes. Now that I'm home, I want to stay. I want to get to know this new version of my dad and hopefully work through our issues so we can have a relationship again.

But then I glance at Julian, whose jaw is tight.

"If my fiancé will have me," I say, half joking.

I glance up at him and flutter my lashes playfully, and his jaw untightens. And if I'm not mistaken, a hint of a smile quirks in the corner of his mouth. His small smile shouldn't send butterflies fluttering through my belly, yet it does. I need to be careful because my body is clearly refusing to get on the same page with the rest of me.

"I'll have to find my place here, like anyone else just hired," I say to both of them when Julian doesn't respond, "but if Kingston is a good fit and Julian's okay with me staying on, I'd like to work for Kingston." I glance at Julian, meeting his gaze. "It's our family business."

Julian clenches his jaw once again, understanding the words I'm not saying. He might be close with my dad, but at the end of the day, only one of us has the last name Kingston.

Breaking eye contact with him, I look back at my dad. "I'm not going anywhere regardless of the outcome."

We have a long way to go to mend our relationship, but I'm done running from my past. I never should've stayed away as long as I did, and now that I'm home and it's clear my dad has changed his ways, I don't want to be stubborn and miss out on having a relationship with him. I thought I had many years with my mom, but I was wrong. Life can be taken from us at any moment.

A bright smile spreads across my dad's face, and before I know what's happening, he's engulfing me in a hug. It's the third time he's hugged me since I've been back, and I don't know how I went all these years without them.

"I love you, sweetie," he murmurs. "And I'm so glad you're finally home."

When we separate, Dad clears his throat. "Okay then, instead of you working directly with the marketing department, I think it would be best if you work on this floor. I have an office for you that I had maintenance clean out last night. With me planning to announce my replacement at the end of the year, that only gives me less than six months to decide. To keep it fair, I've decided to see how you both handle the situations given to you, starting with Ronan Flynn."

"The musician?" Julian asks as I try to figure out who that is.

Thanks to living in the UK, I'm put at a disadvantage regarding all things American.

"Yep," Dad says. "Selene's daughter, Ingrid, works for his record label. He's been blowing up on the charts, and he's a hometown boy, born and raised in Rosemary. After confirming he's got a good reputation, I'd like to get him on board for a collaboration. Which is where you two come in."

Dad crosses his arms over his chest and grins like he's enjoying this way too much. "You'll both present your ideas to the team on Friday."

Julian chuckles. "Sounds good." He leans over and kisses my cheek, shocking the hell out of me. "I'm going to head to my office to do some work. I'll let you spend some time with your dad."

I watch him saunter out, trying not to notice how nice his ass looks in his charcoal-gray pants, knowing this was strategic on his part so he can get a head start while I'm stuck here, hanging out with my dad. But that's fine because his little bit of a head start isn't going to mean shit when I present the better idea on Friday.

"All right, Anastasia," Dad says, shaking me from my thoughts, "you ready to see your office?"

"More than ready."

Ten

ANASTASIA

"It's late."

Dad's voice has me jumping out of my skin as I look up from my computer and control my breathing to slow my heart rate.

"It is?"

I glance at the clock. Six o'clock. Hardly late. Hell, some days at Benson, six o'clock was when I would down some espresso, get a second wind, and work until ten or eleven.

"Your fiancé left over an hour ago," he points out. "Did you two not carpool this morning?"

Shit, I didn't even consider that.

"We weren't sure how it would all work with today being my first day. I didn't want to hold him up."

"Go home," Dad says gently. "Tomorrow is another day."

I want to argue, but I bite my tongue, knowing he's testing me. This is what he doesn't want—his CEO working until all hours of the night instead of being home with their family.

"You're right," I agree, saving what I was working on so I can work on it at home. It's not like I'm actually going home to spend time with my fake fiancé.

When I get home, I park inside the garage and notice Julian is home since his car and truck are both present. I close the garage door and then head in through the mudroom that's located off the side of the kitchen, immediately getting a whiff of what smells like garlic.

Mmm, Italian.

My stomach rumbles, reminding me that I didn't eat lunch or dinner because I was too busy working on my pitch for the Ronan Flynn collaboration.

I'm expecting Julian to be at the table with takeout, so I'm taken aback when I instead find him standing in front of the stove, dressed in a pair of black sweatpants and a white shirt, his feet bare, stirring something in a pot.

"Are you cooking?" I blurt out before I can stop myself.

He glances my way and chuckles. "No, I just thought it would be fun to pour a bunch of ingredients into a pot and watch them boil."

I roll my eyes at his sarcasm. "I didn't know you could cook."

"You don't know a lot of things about me," he says dryly.

"Touché."

"When I was growing up, my mom said everyone should know how to cook, clean, and do laundry," he says, continuing to stir whatever's in the pot. "She made my sister and me cook with her several times a week, clean our own bedrooms and bathroom, and do our own laundry." He shrugs. "I have someone come in to clean and do my laundry now that I can afford it and am busy with work, but I prefer to cook for myself rather than go out to eat or order in every night. It's healthier, and it tastes better."

I stare at him in shock and awe at how normal that sounds. I've never done any of the above, but I'm not about to mention that and sound like a spoiled brat. It's not that I think I'm above it, but unlike his mom, mine never considered cooking, cleaning, or doing laundry a teachable life lesson. She came from money, and from the time I was born, all of that stuff was always handled.

Unlike my friends though, I only had a nanny when it was necessary—when Mom would attend engagements with my dad that I didn't go to. She preferred to devote her time to me, and I believe that's why we were so close. She was my best friend, and I miss her so much.

"So, you think your cooking tastes better, huh?" I say, poking the beast. "Clearly, you've never been to Enzo's in London. It has three Michelin stars." I walk over to the stove and look into the pot, spotting the tomato sauce. "One of them was for his sauce alone." I'm making that up, but Julian doesn't know that.

"No, I've never been to Enzo's," he admits, taking the spoon and lifting it to my mouth. "And I've obviously never been given an award for my food, but I have been told my sauce is delicious." As the last word rolls off his tongue, the spoon touches my lips, and I still in my spot.

"Blow," he murmurs, his green eyes filled with mischief.

I do as he said, blowing lightly on the spoon for a few seconds before I part my lips and he slides the spoon into my mouth. Julian feeding me his sauce shouldn't be such a turn-on, yet I find myself squeezing my legs together, trying to find a little bit of relief.

I close my lips and suck on the wooden spoon, and fresh garlic, several different herbs, sweet tomatoes, and so many other flavors instantly burst against my taste buds.

"Holy shit," I murmur. "That's ..."

"Orgasmic?" Julian finishes for me, raising a brow. "Yeah, I know." He smirks and goes back to stirring the sauce. "I've been told."

I don't know why, but the thought of him feeding other women and them comparing it to orgasms has me seeing green with jealousy. I've never been that type of woman, never cared enough about a man to feel that kind of emotion, and the fact that I'm feeling it because of Julian and his damn sauce doesn't sit well with me. I'm supposed to be focusing on beating him out of the CEO position, not having *foodgasms*.

"Whatever," I mutter, walking away.

Before I can get far though, he grabs my wrist and pulls me back to him, my body pressing against his. My hands land on his muscular pecs, and it doesn't go unnoticed how hard his body is. Was it only a few days ago that I was wrapped around him, kissing him like he was the breath of air I needed to survive?

"Have you had dinner yet?" he asks, his hand sliding down my side and landing on the curve of my hip.

The intimate gesture feels so good that all rational thought flies out the window.

When I shake my head, unable to form words, he nods once and says, "Go get comfortable. Dinner will be ready soon."

I should tell him that I'm good and then hide out in my bedroom, away from his mesmerizing emerald eyes, hypnotizing scent, and orgasmic freaking sauce, where it's safe, but instead, I find myself agreeing.

After I've rinsed the day off and changed into a pair of comfy leggings and a tank top, I make my way back downstairs, where I find Julian pouring me a glass of red wine to go with the delicious-looking spaghetti and meatballs on my plate. There's also a salad and ...

"Are these homemade?" I ask, pointing to the fluffy garlic knots.

"Yep," he says, pouring himself three fingers of scotch, which I immediately recognize as Kingston's from the crown on the label—the company's signature logo my dad designed many years ago. "Today was stressful, and I find cooking is a good way to relax."

"Why was it stressful?" I ask, taking a sip of my wine.

"Spent most of the day putting out fires," he says, taking a bite of a garlic knot and then washing it down with his scotch. "How was your day?" he asks.

"Productive," I admit, noting how domestic this feels. "I got my office set up and spent the afternoon working on my pitch."

He nods. "Oh, since we're playing house, Ryder and his fiancée are doing a destination wedding in Hawaii." He rolls his eyes, and I'm not sure if it's because he's against the wedding or Hawaii. "Everyone, including your dad and Selene, will be there, so I need you to plan to go." He thinks thoughtfully for a moment, then adds, "I'll have Josie sync our calendars. That way, we can keep track of our commitments."

"Ryder's the CFO, right?" I ask, remembering him from my research.

"Yeah, and my best friend," he says, taking a bite of his food.

Of course he is. Apparently, I've stepped into a damn gentleman's club. Sure, women work there as well. Most of them are in other departments or are assistants. A few are managers or supervisors, but the majority of the upper-level team is made up of men.

"What's that look for?" he questions.

"What look?"

"As soon as I told you Ryder's my best friend, you got a sour look on your face."

Damn it, I forgot how observant this man is.

"I just noticed that a lot of upper-level management are men. I didn't realize how sexist my dad was."

Maybe that's why he doesn't feel I'm a good fit for the position, which means I don't stand a chance against Julian and everything I'm doing is pointless.

The thought has my hackles rising and motivates me that much more. If I do everything better than Julian, go beyond the expectations, Dad will have no choice but to pick me or risk looking sexist.

Julian scoffs. "Your dad is not sexist. Besides, I'm the one who handles the majority of the hiring."

"So, you're sexist," I poke, making Julian glare my way. "Oh, c'mon. Every three-letter position is filled by a man," I point out.

"That's not true," he argues.

"Oh, really? Let's see here. CEO: man," I start, ticking it off, using my pointer finger. "COO: man." My middle finger goes up. "CFO: man, CMO: man, and CTO: also a man." With all five fingers in the air, I give him a condescending wave and a matching smile. "When I get the CEO position, I don't know how all you *men* are going to handle taking orders from a woman in charge."

"You know, Red," he says, annoyance and anger dripping with every word, "if you bow out now, I can assure you that you'll have the spot as the COO, and then there'll be a woman with three letters."

"Ha!" I bark out a laugh. "That sounds to me like you're scared. As you should be," I say, taking a sip of my wine and locking eyes with him. "And unlike your false promises, when I become CEO, I'll *consider* keeping you in your position."

I stand despite wanting so badly to eat my delicious food. "I've lost my appetite."

I walk by him, stopping when I'm right next to him.

"One thing about working with men is that you have no idea how crazy a woman can be when she wants something," I say, leaning down and using the table to hold myself up so I don't touch him. "The thing about spiders is that they're quiet, so you never see them coming. And before you realize they're there, they've already attacked and left you for dead. Be careful, Julian. Like you said, I'm venomous. Let this be your warning. I'm coming after you, and I'm not going to hold back."

"KNOCK, KNOCK."

I glance up and find my dad standing in the doorway of my office. I was so lost in what I was doing that I didn't even hear him approach.

"Hey, Dad," I say, smiling through my annoyance at my concentration being broken. "What's up?"

"I, uh …" He clears his throat, and I can't help noticing he looks nervous. A million thoughts go through my head, but when he speaks, I'm a bit confused. "I was wondering if you might want to have lunch with me."

He wants to eat with me?

I look at the time and see it's noon. Technically, I can take a lunch, but ...

"I'm in the middle of working on my pitch," I tell him.

With us only having a couple of days before the meeting, he must know we're going to spend every second possible on it. Yet he pretty much demanded I go home early last night, and now, he wants me to take a break to have lunch.

His face falls, but he nods in understanding.

"No worries," he says. "Another day."

He forces a smile and then retreats, leaving me alone.

I turn back to my laptop screen and continue to work, but I can't get the sad look on my dad's face out of my head. And the way he was nervous to ask me to eat with him ...

And then Julian's words come back to me. *But every Wednesday, she came to the office and brought him lunch, and every week, he told her he was too busy. Eventually, she stopped coming.*

And it hits me. Today is Wednesday, and I just did the same thing to my dad that he had done to my mom. He's trying to right his wrongs, but he's right. Instead of doing the opposite of the man I resented, I've become him. Only I justify it because I refuse to get married and have kids, so I'm not hurting anyone but myself—and now him.

Grabbing my card and phone, I rush out of the office and over to the sub shop we used to frequent when I was little and order our favorites, hoping it's still his. Then, I go straight to his office, hoping to find him there. When I find his office empty, my heart sinks. But then he steps out of his private bathroom, and our eyes meet.

"I bought us subs," I tell him, lifting the bag as proof. "If you'd still like to have lunch with me."

His eyes turn glassy, and a beautiful smile spreads across his face that makes me hate myself for going six years without seeing him. Yeah, he fucked up. But he's human, and after we lost Mom, we only had each other. But instead, I left, thinking I was punishing him—without realizing I was punishing us both.

"That would be wonderful. How about in the conference room?" he suggests despite him having a table in his office.

"That sounds perfect."

Eleven

JULIAN

"Hey, Josie, have you seen Samuel?" I ask after not finding him in his office.

I have a bunch of contracts that need his approval and signature, and I want to get them back to our legal team so I can work on this damn pitch.

"He's in the conference room," she says, "having lunch with Anastasia."

I stop in my tracks at her words. "In the conference room?"

He hasn't had lunch in there since …

"Yep, and today's Wednesday," she notes, having been here long enough to know what that day symbolizes.

I walk around the corner and stop when I see Samuel and Red sitting together at the table, eating their lunch. She throws her head back in laughter, and even though I can't hear her, I imagine the melodic sound that comes from her. She smiles softly at her dad, and my heart clenches in my chest. Only a few short days ago, she was smiling at me, laughing with me, kissing me, and I was imagining what it might feel like to settle down.

Now, despite the fact that I'm still attracted to her, she's the enemy, and regardless of what she told her dad about us not having any hard feelings, I know damn well if I get the CEO position, Anastasia will not take it well.

I watch as she rests her hand on her dad's arm and her eyes crinkle in happiness. A part of me is happy for them, happy that Samuel finally has his daughter back after all these years. I know how much he missed her. The hurt that would cross over his features when he'd talk about her.

But another part of me—the selfish part—knows this is a problem. It doesn't matter what I do, what pitches I come up with, how much I prove that I'm clearly the better candidate to take his place as CEO, Anastasia has something I don't have—his blood running through her veins.

She said it herself—she's his daughter. He might consider me a son, but she's his flesh and blood, and there's no fucking way I can compete with that. It isn't going to stop me from giving it my all, just like I've given this company everything of me for the past twenty years, but if she gets the position I've earned because of her last name, I don't think I could continue to work here.

I shake those thoughts from my head. There's no point in driving myself crazy with what-ifs. Once Samuel makes his decision, I'll go from there. The fact is, I've worked my ass off over the years, and even though I don't have a fancy degree, I have the experience, and many companies would jump at the chance to hire me. They've tried to recruit me on more than one occasion, but I love working at Kingston, I'm loyal to this company, and I've always thought I would stay here until I retired.

Still needing the signatures, I leave them on his desk with a sticky note and then go back to my desk to delve into my idea. I'm not gonna lie. It's been a while since I've been on this side of things. The marketing team usually handles the pitches, and I'm the one to approve them. Which is another reason I'm concerned. I did my research on Anastasia once I found out who she really was, and to say she ran the marketing team at Benson would be putting it mildly. According to a few of her former colleagues I spoke with, she was practically running the company, and now, Victoria Benson is struggling to replace her.

She was clearly an asset there and knows what she's doing. If I want any chance of beating her out of the position, my idea needs to be better than whatever she comes up with. If Samuel sees I'm the best fit for CEO, he'll have no choice but to give it to me. He might be on this whole family-man kick, but he's always been known to be fair.

I'm neck deep in my research when Ryder knocks on my door.

"Hey, we still on for tonight?" he asks, looking at me with hope in his eyes.

Tonight? And then I remember ... I agreed to have the guys over to watch the baseball game tonight.

"Yeah," I tell him, not wanting to bail since this is his weekly break from his controlling fiancée.

Why he stays with her, I'll never know. It's obvious he's so unhappy. They met a few months back, and she bulldozed her way into his life. Even though he seemed into her at first, she quickly showed her true colors, so I was shocked when they announced their engagement and he bought a mansion for them to move into, and I was even more shocked when a wedding invitation arrived, dated for this summer.

"Okay, cool," he mutters. "I'll see you later."

"Wait," I say. "Is everything okay? If you need to talk ..."

He sighs and then comes inside, closing the door behind him.

When he sits in the visitor chair across from me, he swallows thickly and shakes his head. "Nora was pregnant."

"Was?" I question, making sure I heard him correctly.

"Yeah," he chokes out. "She didn't want anyone to know because it would look bad, her being pregnant out of wedlock." He sighs. "You know our type of families. She didn't want people to judge her. It's why I proposed. We were planning to be married before she started to show."

"And what happened?"

"She miscarried," he says, his glassy eyes meeting mine. "She wasn't that far along, but it still sucked."

"Of course it did," I tell him, getting up and pouring us each two fingers of scotch.

He takes a sip of his drink and leans back in his seat. "She wanted to wait until she was in her second trimester to tell anyone. I guess that's the norm."

"I'm sorry, man," I tell him, sitting back down.

I might not like Nora, but I care about Ryder, and I hate that he's been dealing with this on his own. I mean, he has Nora, but she's so damn selfish that I doubt she gives a shit about his feelings.

"Thanks," he says. "I should've said something, but it's all just been a mess, and I'm so used to hiding everything because of my family."

Ryder comes from a ridiculously wealthy, high-class family. They're practically Texas royalty. It doesn't help that his brother is the governor and plans to eventually run for president. So, everything Ryder does is watched and criticized.

"You mentioned you proposed because she was pregnant," I prompt. "But since she's not anymore ..."

"Yeah." He throws back the rest of his scotch and sets the glass on the desk. "She was doing bad after the miscarriage, and the only thing that seemed to make her happy was planning the wedding. I was waiting for a good time to cancel the engagement, but then ... fuck," he curses under his breath and tilts his head up to look at the ceiling for several seconds before he glances back at me.

"We hadn't had sex since the miscarriage. I didn't want to lead her on, but she begged me to take her away for the weekend. Said it would help her mentally. I'd been drinking, and one thing led to another. I swear I used a condom."

Oh fuck. "Tell me you didn't get her pregnant again."

"I went to call off the wedding a week ago, but before I could, she told me she was pregnant. I went with her to the doctor yesterday, and he confirmed it."

"Shit, man."

"Yeah. I looked it up. You know a woman can only get pregnant, like, three days a month?"

"Really?"

"Yeah," he repeats. "I don't think it's a coincidence she begged me to go away that weekend. Said she was feeling low and needed to get away. I felt bad, so I took her away. We ended up at a tiki bar, both of us shit-faced, and I fucked up. I gave in and had sex with her. But here's the thing: even as drunk as I was, I know I used protection, Julian. I wouldn't risk that shit happening again."

"You think she trapped you?"

Holy fuck, this chick is crazier than I thought.

"Doesn't fucking matter now," Ryder says. "She's pregnant with my baby, and the wedding is in a couple of weeks."

"Are you sure it's yours?" I question.

"I won't find out for another few weeks. I considered postponing the wedding until the paternity test could be done, but that will create a fucking mess, so I'm just going along with it, and if it turns out this baby isn't mine, I'm kicking Nora out on her ass."

I pour him another two fingers of scotch, and he throws it back and stands.

"Do me a favor and keep this between us," he says before he opens the door.

"Of course," I tell him. "And for what it's worth, you'll be a damn good dad."

"Thanks."

I spend the next couple of hours working on my pitch, and when my alarm goes off, indicating that I need to go so I can be home before the guys arrive, I shut everything down and take off.

"DID YOU SEE THAT?" TIM YELLS. "THAT WAS CLEARLY a fucking strike! That umpire is a joke!"

He takes a swig of his beer, and I chuckle at how worked up he gets. Like most of the male species, I enjoy sports, but unlike Tim, I don't take them as seriously as he does.

"How much you gonna lose?" I ask, scooping a chip into the queso dip I made.

"Enough," Tim grunts.

He looks like he's about to say something else, but his words are halted as my fake fiancée saunters through the house. She's dressed in a sexy royal-blue dress that wraps around her body, the front dipping just low enough to show off her perky breasts. Her hair is up in some kind of knot, putting her slim neck on display, and she's sporting tall black heels with the signature red soles that somehow make her legs look even longer and more toned. Images of her wrapping her legs around my neck while I devour her pussy surface, but I quickly force them away before I end up hard right in front of the guys.

When Anastasia notices that she's attracted the attention of five guys, she stops in her place and stares back momentarily, like a deer caught in headlights. Her eyes settle on me, and at first, I'm confused as to why she's looking like she needs my help—until I remember that aside from Ryder, everyone thinks we're really engaged and in love.

"Hey, Red," I say, standing and walking over to her. I lean in and give her a soft kiss on the corner of her mouth and try like hell to ignore the way her floral, fruity scent affects me. "How was your day?" I murmur loud enough that everyone can hear me playing the doting fiancé, but soft enough that it looks like I'm being sweet and not playing a part.

"Good," she rasps. "You?"

I hold back my chuckle at how badly she sucks at this. I'm not saying I'm an expert at relationships by any means, but at least I don't look like someone's holding me at gunpoint.

"Good," I parrot. "I'm sure you've met most of the guys, but let me introduce you, just in case." I slide my arm around her waist and pull her into my side as I walk her into the living room.

"Ryder Du Ponte ..."

"CFO," she finishes. "Tim Thorne, CTO," she says next, obviously having done her research. "Evan Sanchez, CMO." She plasters on a fake smile. "And my dear fiancé, the COO. Looks like the boys' club is together. The only one missing is my father ..."

"Oh, he doesn't join us anymore," Tim says, not catching on to her sarcasm. "He's been MIA ever since he met Selene."

Anastasia looks like she wants to say something condescending, but instead, she simply smiles and nods.

"That's nice. So, what are you guys up to tonight?"

The sight of her trying to play nice with men she clearly hates due to their gender alone would be comical if I wasn't one of the men she hated.

The guys all stare at her—out of shock or discomfort, I have no clue—so I answer her. "We're watching the game." I nod toward the baseball game that's still going in the background. "We ordered pizza and wings. It should be here soon if you want to join us." I turn her toward me and tip her chin so she's looking at me. "I could start that lesson in sports I promised you."

I smirk, knowing the last thing she wants is to sit with me and the guys and watch baseball. "What do you say, babe? Pizza, beer, and baseball with your man?"

She blinks rapidly several times and then glares, and if looks could kill, I'd be dead on the floor. "I wish I could, *babe*. But we have our pitches due Friday. Are you already done with yours?"

"It's not rocket science," I say, playing off the fact that I still have no damn clue what I'm going to do. I was trying to put something together all day, but I'm having a major creative block ... or maybe I'm just overthinking shit. "I've secured dozens of deals." I shrug nonchalantly. "I'll be ready for Friday, no problem."

"Really?" she says, the challenge evident in her tone. "Since you seem to think you have this in the bag, why don't we make this interesting?"

"What do you have in mind?" I ask, resting my hands on her hips and tugging her toward me.

"If I win, you have to ..." She looks around thoughtfully, and then her eyes light up. "You have to cook me dinner for a month."

I chuckle at how adorable she is, wanting something as normal as home-cooked meals. The truth is, she doesn't need to win a bet to get me to cook for her. I'd do it willingly—every damn day for the rest of our lives if she let me. That admission should scare the hell out of me because she's supposed to be the enemy, yet I still can't stop wanting her.

Fuck, I'm so screwed with this woman.

"And what do I get if I win?" I murmur.

"What do you want?" she volleys.

"You," I say without thought.

Her eyes widen, and she glances behind her at the guys nervously, reminding me we have an audience. I have no clue why I just said I want her when, technically, I already have her due to our fake engagement, but I need to fix this before I blow our cover.

"I want you alone for a weekend," I clarify. "A romantic weekend away. Just the two of us."

She sighs in relief, but to the guys, she probably sounds like she's in awe over how romantic her fiancé is.

"Sure," she says, extending her hand to shake on it, not realizing that I'm being dead serious.

I take her hand in mine and pull her toward me until our bodies are flush. Then, I kiss her before she can stop me, relishing in her soft lips.

"What was that for?" she whispers so nobody can hear her but me.

"Sealed the bet with a kiss," I mutter, knowing it's in my best interest to stay away from her unless it's necessary, but also realizing I can't stop the gravitational pull I feel toward her.

She's threatening my career and my future, yet I still want her. Since I refuse to acknowledge how crazy that makes me, I'm sticking to the whole *Keep your friends close and your enemies closer*. And since Anastasia is my enemy, I'm going to work extra hard at keeping her very, very close.

"So, by creating a familial atmosphere, I think Ronan Flynn will be more inclined to sign. He is, after all, a family man."

Anastasia smiles at the room, and everyone nods in agreement. The woman hasn't been here more than a week, and she's already got everyone eating out of her damn hands.

After she left the other night to hide out in her room while the guys and I finished our game and devoured our weight in pizza and wings, they mentioned no less than a dozen times how hot my fiancée was and that her feistiness only made her that much sexier. I didn't disagree with them, but I think what rubbed me the wrong way was the fact that she wasn't actually mine.

And then yesterday, I saw her having lunch with half the tech department and several of the marketing people. She thinks kissing ass is going to give her the upper hand, but I've been working with these people for years, and their loyalty lies with me.

"Good job," Samuel says, smiling at his daughter. "Does anyone have any questions?"

When nobody speaks up, he says, "Julian, you're up."

I stand and walk over to the head of the table, pulling my slideshow up. Unlike Anastasia, who supplied every team member with a portfolio of info, including a bunch of data she had run—which was overkill—I don't need any of that shit because I've got this on my own.

No, my idea isn't family friendly, but it will get the deal signed. Because what Anastasia didn't uncover in her research is that while Ronan might be a family man, he's also a businessman.

"Ronan Flynn is a musician, and one of his recent investments involves a club called Craic. He's recently opened one in Houston and is planning to open another in Vegas next month. He's put a lot of money into this investment, and he spends a lot of his time there. I think we keep it simple. We ask for a meeting at his club and lay our collab idea on the table for him, explaining that it will be mutually beneficial since we'll supply our products for his clubs at a lower premium."

Before anyone can say anything, Anastasia speaks up. "That's it? That's your idea? Go clubbing with the guy?"

"Not clubbing," I say dryly, annoyed at the way she's mocking my idea. "We have the meeting at his club. It's the perfect way to create the ambience. What better place to discuss a liquor collab than at a club that serves liquor?"

"Oh my God." She snorts. "How have you managed to keep this business running all these years? Trying to secure a potential client isn't an excuse to party."

"It's better than your idea," I argue. "A luncheon? This isn't the *Housewives of Houston*. He's not a trophy wife, looking to have tea in the garden and gossip about the latest cheating scandal. He's a businessman, and businessmen have business meetings all over, including at a club."

"Seriously?" Anastasia screeches, but before she can continue, her dad steps in between us.

"Obviously, we have two people who are passionate about their ideas," Samuel says with a chuckle. "Let's take a break, and we'll reconvene after lunch."

Everyone shuffles out of the room, no doubt happy to get the hell out of here and away from the tension.

"You are so sexist!" Anastasia shouts once it's only the three of us.

"I didn't mean it like that," I say, recognizing my poor word choice despite my intent not being wrong. "But you can't deny that men and women are different. Most men don't do luncheons and tea. *Women* do. Men prefer sporting events and dinners. That's not me being sexist. It's me being a smart business*person*. I research them and focus on how to hook them in. You're so busy focusing on the familial aspect that you're not thinking clearly."

"Okay, okay," Samuel says. "You both make good points, but I think in this case, we're going to go with the luncheon idea. I can invite Selene, and we'll show Ronan what it means to be part of the Kingston family." He glances at Anastasia and adds, "The new and improved family."

She smiles softly, and it takes everything in me not to chuck my laptop across the room because what the fuck?!

"This is a liquor company," I point out. "Clubs and liquor go hand in hand."

"That doesn't mean we have to be unprofessional," Anastasia adds.

"We've held many meetings at clubs and restaurants."

"I know," Samuel says, "but in this case, I think it's best if we give Anastasia's idea a try. If it doesn't work—"

"Then it's done," I finish. "Because we all know you only have one shot to draw in a client." I step back and raise my hands. "But, hey, you do what you feel is best. It's your company."

I turn around and stalk out of the room, and as I leave, I hear Samuel calling my name, but I'm too pissed off to answer him. Instead of going back to my office, I go to Ryder's.

"That was something," he says when I walk into his office without knocking and slam the door behind me.

"That was fucking bullshit. Samuel's so busy trying to kiss his daughter's ass that he's not thinking straight."

"I take it, he chose her idea over yours?"

"Of course he did," I say, dropping into the visitor seat across from him. "And he's making a mistake. A guy like Ronan isn't the luncheon type."

Ryder pours us each two fingers of scotch and slides one my way. "So, what's the plan?"

"What do you mean?" I down my drink in one gulp and slam it on the desk.

"You've been handling shit for years, Julian. You know what you're doing. Are you going to let Kingston lose a profitable deal because Samuel's gone soft?"

Am I? A part of me wants to sit back and watch Anastasia fail. It's not that her idea is bad, but it's not right for this client. She's still thinking like she's in London. Maybe luncheons are how they do things there, but here, we handle it differently.

"What do you think I should do?"

"Get to him first." Ryder shrugs. "If you just so happen to run into him at the club and happen to mention the collaboration ..."

"And he *happens* to agree," I finish. "If this works, Anastasia is going to be so pissed."

"Maybe, but do you really care? It's not like your relationship with her is real."

"True." But even as I say the word, my gut churns at the thought of going behind her back.

If I do this, it's going to draw a clear line in the sand, one I don't think we can come back from. Am I willing to risk that? The answer should be glaringly obvious. She's nobody to me. A fake fiancée I hired to help me get my promotion. Yet, even as I think the words, I know I'm lying to myself.

Ryder pulls out his phone and types for a few seconds and then turns the phone around so I can see the screen. "Ronan will be there tomorrow night. He's performing."

"Fuck, this can go so wrong ..."

"Or you seal the deal."

"She's going to kill me."

"All's fair in love and war." Ryder pours us both another drink, and we clink glasses.

"In this case, I have a feeling I'm starting a war."

Twelve

ANASTASIA

"Hey, Josie. Have you seen my dad?"

"I don't think he's in yet, hon, but Julian's here."

"Oh, he is?" I say, surprised he showed up today.

We were able to secure a luncheon with Ronan today, so everyone's been all hands on deck to get everything ready. I didn't see Julian all weekend, and I just assumed he was hiding out, licking his wounds.

"Yeah, he's in a meeting with Ronan Flynn," she says, waggling her brows. "Girl, that man is even more scrumptious in person. And that voice. Forget singing. He can just talk to me all day, and I'll be happy."

She giggles like a schoolgirl with a crush while I try to figure out why the hell Julian is in a meeting with Ronan Flynn when the luncheon isn't until later today.

There's only one reason why he would be meeting with him at nine in the morning.

I stalk down the hall and knock on the door, ready to kill my fake fucking fiancé.

"Anastasia," Julian says when he opens the door. "Perfect timing. I was just about to find you. I'd like you to meet Ronan Flynn. He's going to be partnering with Kingston."

"Nice to meet you," I grit out, trying to remain professional.

"Likewise," he says, shaking my hand. "I expect our partnership will be very fruitful on both ends."

Julian offers to walk Ronan out to the lobby, letting me know he'll be right back.

When he returns a few minutes later, I slow clap as he walks in and closes the door. "Congrats. You win."

He sighs and shakes his head. "I know you're pissed but—"

"You played dirty!" I poke him in the chest.

"I got it done."

"You—"

A knock cuts me off, followed by my dad opening the door.

"Everything okay in here?" Dad asks, his brows furrowed in concern.

"Everything's good," Julian says. "Anastasia and I were just celebrating. Ronan signed. The deal's done."

"Wow. Good job, you two." Dad shakes Julian's hand and then hugs me. "Does that mean the luncheon is off?"

"Yeah," I choke out, "it's unnecessary."

"Selene and I were looking forward to it, but I'm glad you guys got him to sign. And I'm proud of you for working together." He grins wide. "This calls for a celebratory dinner. Tonight at Mario's, seven o'clock?"

"Sounds good," Julian says, sliding his arm across my waist while I envision reaching over and grabbing the pen off his desk and stabbing him in the shoulder with it.

Once my dad is gone, I pull away from him. "I can't believe you went behind my back! We agreed on the luncheon!"

"No!" he barks, getting in my face. "You and your father ganged up on me."

"You're just pissed you didn't get your way. A good leader is a team player."

"A good leader does their research and gets shit done," he argues. "I saw an opportunity and took it. And it worked. That's why I'm the COO—because I get shit done."

"Yet you didn't tell my dad how you got it done. This is why he's reluctant to hire someone single. Partying with a potential client at a club isn't how you do business."

"When the potential client is a musician who owns a club, it is. And before your dad went soft, he not only would've condoned it, but probably suggested it as well.

"You might not like it, but you're living in a man's world, Red, and the sooner you realize it, the quicker you'll be put into the game. It's not sexist. It's facts. And if you don't start thinking like a man, you're going to be left sitting on the bench."

He walks around the desk and drops into his seat. "Do you want to meet at the house and ride together or meet at the restaurant?"

"Fuck you, asshole. It's game on, and if you think I'm going to take this lying down, you have another thing coming. I'm about to blow your *man's world* apart!"

"I MEAN, I GET WHERE YOU'RE COMING FROM," PAIGE says over video chat.

I've just spent the last hour ranting to her about Julian going behind my back, and once I was done, I asked for her honest opinion. But I have a feeling in about ten seconds, I'm going to regret doing so.

"But I also have to agree with him," she says slowly, trying to soften the blow. "A luncheon is something you'd do here for the fifty-year-old men we deal with, but for a hip, young musician who owns clubs ..." She shrugs. "I'm not saying it wasn't risky, but I can see why he did it."

Damn it, I know she's right, but I hate that Julian went behind my back. He could've come to me and talked to me, explained where he was coming from ...

"And you know damn well if he had come to you, you would've gotten defensive and shut him down," Paige adds, as if she can hear my thoughts.

"Do you think my dad only agreed to the luncheon because of me?" I ask as the reality of the situation hits.

"What do you think?" Paige volleys, refusing to give me an out.

"I think if I wasn't stuck on trying to convince my dad I'm all about family, I would've been on board with the club idea," I admit.

"And what about your dad?" she pushes.

"I think between being in love and trying to get in my good graces, he wasn't thinking clearly. The man who's built Kingston to be one of the biggest liquor companies in the world would've done what needed to be done, not taken the safe route ... and definitely not with a luncheon."

I sigh, hating that Julian was right. "But that doesn't change the fact that my fake fiancé went behind my back and then told me I'm not 'man' enough to hang with the men. I'm going to show him that fucking with a woman is way scarier than dealing with a man."

"Oh Lord," Paige says with a laugh. "What are you going to do?"

"I don't know yet," I say, "but once I figure it out, I'll let you know after I do it."

"After?" She quirks a brow.

"Yeah, *after*. So you can't talk me out of it."

"If you're going to request my presence, it would help if I knew where you were."

I glance behind me at the masculine voice and then take the shot, watching as the seven ball disappears into the pocket.

Ignoring Julian's statement, I search the table for my next shot and then lean over and take it. The six ball goes in, and when I glance back again, Julian's heated gaze is on my ass.

"I was looking for you, but when I checked in this room, I got distracted by the pool table."

I scour the table for my next shot, and when I find it, I walk over and take it. The three ball goes in, and when I stand up and turn, ready to find my next shot, I'm met with Julian's hard front pressing up against me. His hands land on either side of my body, caging me in, and his mouth is so close to mine that if I move forward an inch, our lips will meet.

"You play pool?" he asks.

"My freshman year of college, I dated a pool shark."

He lifts me onto the edge of the table and takes the stick out of my hand, dropping it onto the felt.

He parts my thighs and stands between them.

This close, I can smell his spicy scent, and I hate the way it does shit to me.

"What's up, Red? What did you need to talk about?"

I lick my lips, and his gaze homes in on my mouth for several seconds before he ascends to meet my eyes.

"You were right," I say, cursing my traitorous body for the way it reacts to him. My voice is far too breathy, I can feel my nipples hardening under the material of the dress I put on for dinner, and if he were to touch the apex of my legs, he would find me wet.

Julian blinks several times and then says, "What?"

"I said, you were right." I lift my chin, holding my head up high. "I'm not too proud to admit when someone else was right, and you were right. At Benson, I dealt with mostly older clients, and luncheons were the way to go. Knowing that my dad wants someone who's more family oriented, I went with the safe route. But it wasn't the right route."

"Thanks," he says with a nod. "I appreciate that."

"It doesn't change the fact that you're a sexist asshole who went behind your fake fiancée's back, but you were right." I push at his chest, silently telling him to back up so I can walk away, but he doesn't budge.

"You're wrong," he says. "The previous CMO and CTO were both women. Kimberly left when she was offered a better job that would allow her to climb the ladder quicker, and Nathalie had a baby."

I glare at him, and he clarifies, "We held her position for months after she gave birth while she was on maternity leave, and then we had to find her replacement when she decided she wanted to stay home indefinitely. Both times, I did the hiring, and it just so happens that it was men who were the most qualified and would fit in best. But had either been a woman, I would've hired her in a heartbeat."

"Whatever," I mutter. "I'm still mad at you."

"Speaking of which," he says, "what do you like to eat?"

"What does that have to do with me being mad at you?"

"Nothing." He laughs. "But I'm hoping that reminding you that you won, which means I'll be cooking dinner for you for the next month, will make you a little less mad."

Oh, right, the bet ...

"I didn't win."

"Your dad picked your idea," he argues.

"Only because I'm his daughter." I roll my eyes. "You had the better idea."

"Does that mean I get to take you away?"

He leans in slightly, encroaching on my personal space, and I imagine how easy it would be for him to push my panties to the side and make me come.

Jesus, Ana! Get a grip. This man is the damn enemy.

"I don't know why you'd want to," I say, a bit confused by his motives. "It's not like you're trying to woo me. This whole thing between us is fake."

At the time we placed the bet, I thought his idea of taking me away was nothing more than a façade to make it look like we were the real deal in front of his friends.

"What if I didn't want it to be?"

"What are you talking about?"

"What if I wanted to explore the possibility of more between us?" he presses. He stands, and his hands land on the tops of my thighs, his touch sending a shiver down my spine. "When you first got here, the attraction was there. If we weren't both vying for the same position ..."

"Then we would've never met, and we wouldn't be fake engaged."

"Maybe." He shrugs. "But here we are. So, what do you say?"

"I say it's probably best to wait until *after* I get the CEO position." I push him harder this time, and he backs up, giving me enough room to jump off the table and walk past him. "I can't imagine you wanting more once I'm your boss."

"We'll see," Julian says with a chuckle as I saunter out of the room, wondering, not for the first time, what the hell I've gotten myself into with this man.

Thirteen

JULIAN

"Fuck!"

It's nine o'clock. Four hours after the alarm was set to go off. I shoot out of the bed and rush to my bathroom to take a quick piss and brush my teeth. I don't have time to shower since my alarm didn't go off, so I put on deodorant and then grab something to wear. I usually wear a suit, but I'm running late, so I throw on a pair of charcoal-gray slacks and a white button-down shirt and call it good.

The house is quiet, so Red must've left already.

I step into the garage and immediately notice one of the tires on my car is flat. I walk closer and see it's not just one, but all of them.

Shit! Looks like I'll have to take my truck today.

Only when I walk over to it, I see the tires on the truck are also all flat. And what's that? I walk over and find a fucking red lipstick imprint on my goddamn window.

Fucking Red! She apologized, admitted I was right, and then turned around and fucked me over. And she's not even trying to hide it.

I pull out my phone to request an Uber, but of course it says it will be a good hour before one can be here. We live in a small town outside the city, so the place isn't exactly crawling with people who need a ride.

I scroll through my Contacts and call Ryder, hoping he's on his way to work and he can swing by and pick me up.

"Hey, everything okay?" he asks, sounding like he's anything but.

"Anastasia deflated all my tires."

He chuckles. "I take it, she wasn't thrilled with you landing the deal behind her back?"

"Even she admitted I did the right thing," I drawl.

"Yet there you are, stuck at home with eight flat tires. I'll be right there."

By the time Ryder picks me up and we get to work, the meeting Samuel requested at dinner last night is over, and I'm fuming.

Since I already know the meeting was to let everyone know the collab with Ronan has been secured, I go straight to my office. About thirty minutes into my morning routine, Josie lets me know Ronan's on the line.

"Do you not have my personal number?" I ask when I answer.

"I do," he admits. "But calling your office gives me a reason to talk to your assistant."

I chuckle. "How's it going?"

"Good. Lush is having their opening tonight, and I wanted to extend an invite to your team. Celebrate our new joint venture."

Lush is a club-slash-restaurant that's opening in Houston. It's known for its high-class clientele, and unless you're somebody or you know somebody, the wait list to get in is months out. They stock Kingston liquor, so I've been to a few of the openings at their other locations. The ambience is chill, and the food is top-notch.

"Sounds good, man. I'll let everyone know."

"Perfect. Reservations are for eight."

"See you then."

We hang up, and I spend the rest of my day working in my office. I call Samuel to let him know about the dinner, and he says he and Selene will be there.

I have lunch with Ryder and invite him to dinner. He says he can go, but Nora is away with her friends for a girls' trip, so she won't be able to make it.

Thank fucking God.

"Is Anastasia driving you to dinner?" Ryder asks on our way to my place.

"Nah, I have someone from the dealership coming to fill my tires. Unless she slit them. Then, they'll have to tow them in to get new tires put on."

THANKFULLY, THE TIRES WEREN'T SLIT, SO WITHIN minutes of the mechanic arriving, all the tires are back to the way they belong.

Since the reservations aren't until later, I take a shower, get dressed in my suit, and then spend the afternoon reading while waiting for my fiancée to get home.

She works late most nights, but my hope is that she arrives on time tonight since I have a surprise waiting for her. Just a little thank-you for deflating my tires and making me miss our meeting.

Fourteen

ANASTASIA

Today has been great. Not only has Julian stayed the hell away from me—I must admit, after deflating his tires, I was expecting him to come for me—but the agency approved Kingston to move forward with the childcare program. I can't wait to tell my dad tomorrow.

At first, I started it to give myself a one-up on Julian. But I've learned how many employees have had to take time off or hire expensive nannies so they can come back to work, and now, I'm excited to help make this idea come to fruition. I have no plans to have kids anytime soon, if ever, but it's nice to know how many people will use this service, knowing their babies are somewhere safe and they can see them while at work.

It's a little after seven, and I'm planning to order in and then take a long soak in the tub with a large glass of wine. When I pull up to the garage and press the button on the clicker, the garage door doesn't go up. Weird. I press it again, and nothing happens.

Leaving the car parked in the driveway, I grab my purse and make my way around to the front door. I'm searching for my house keys that I never use, so I'm not paying attention when the sprinklers on either side of the sidewalk kick on. They're turned up so high that they soak me from every angle as I scream out in surprise and sprint to the front door, covering my bag that holds my laptop close to my chest.

By the time I make it to the door and open it, I'm beyond drenched and pissed. My initial thought is that I've never noticed the sprinklers on at this time because I always go in through the garage. Then, I close the door behind me and find Julian sitting in the reading chair, his ankle resting on his knee, a book perched in his hand, and a smirk splayed across his face.

Motherfucker!

"Were you playing in the sprinklers?" he asks in an amused tone. "You know we have a pool, yeah?"

"You're an asshole," I hiss, shaking the water off me.

He stands and walks down the hall, then returns a moment later with a towel. And that's when I notice he's dressed to the nines in an all-black suit with an equally black shirt and bow tie, looking like he just stepped off the cover of GQ.

"Going somewhere?" I mutter, snatching the towel from his hand and towel-drying my dripping hair.

"To dinner," he says nonchalantly. "Wanna join me?"

"I'd rather starve than go to dinner with you." I glare.

He chuckles. "Probably for the best." He flicks his wrist and glances at his watch. "Reservations are for eight, and you need a shower." He leans in and sniffs me. "You smell like a wet dog."

DAD

> Missed you at dinner tonight. Julian said you were sick as a dog. Do you need anything?

I'M LYING IN BED, AND I SIT UPRIGHT IN CONFUSION. Dinner? Sick as a ...

Oh, that sneaky bastard! He never said he was meeting my dad for dinner.

ME

> I'm okay. I think it was something I ate.

DAD

> Okay, good. We're meeting tomorrow at 9:00. Ronan mentioned at dinner tonight that he'd like to do something different with our collaboration, and Julian and I agreed. We'll discuss it tomorrow.

Oh my God! I shoot out of bed, ready to murder my fake damn fiancé. Here I thought the sprinklers were payback for me deflating his tires.

ME

> WTF?! You went to dinner without me?

A response comes in seconds later.

JULIAN

I asked you to go. You said you'd rather starve.

ME

Game on, asshole.

JULIAN

Red, I think you've proven you're playing a game you can't win. Probably should surrender before you end up in the doghouse.

I'm going to kill him. No, that would be too easy. I'm going to get him back.

I pace the room, trying to calm my heart rate and think of how to go about it when the perfect idea comes to mind.

I'm going to hell for this.

Straight down, flames a-blazing.

But it'll be worth it.

Julian wants to play dirty and insinuate that because I don't have a dick between my legs, I can't play with the guys. Well, he's about to learn that this woman can play with the big boys—and I'll come out on top. And by the time I'm done, he'll be begging to be taken out of the game.

Yep, I'm going to hell for this.

But it's going to be so worth it.

Fifteen

JULIAN

Last night was fun, but I have to admit, I feel a bit guilty about not being completely honest with Anastasia about the dinner. In my defense, she started this. When I had gone behind her back regarding my meeting with Ronan, it had been for the good of the company. I wasn't trying to play games. But then she deflated all of my damn tires, and I had no choice but to sink to her level. The sprinklers were probably enough payback, and I planned to tell her about the dinner—figuring she'd be forced to quickly get ready or show up, looking like hell—but when she told me she'd rather starve than eat with me, my pettiness reared its ugly head.

After our meeting this morning, I'm going to talk to Anastasia and see if she'll be willing to call it a truce. We both want the CEO position, but there's no reason we have to act like teenagers to get it.

I step into the conference room where the meeting is being held. Only instead of several of the department heads being present, like I thought there would be since we're here to discuss ideas for the Ronan collaboration, it's only Samuel and Anastasia.

"Morning," I tell them, closing the glass door behind me and then having a seat next to Anastasia and across from Samuel.

"Morning," Samuel says, but he barely makes eye contact, and his tone sounds off.

"Okay, now that you're both here, let's get down to it," he continues. "I want our collab with Ronan to go beyond the norm. We need to schedule for him to come in and design his own drink, but we want a marketing plan that will stand out. He made it clear last night that he doesn't do subpar, and neither do we at Kingston.

"Which is where you two come in." His eyes flick between Red and me. "I want something that will go above and beyond, leave the competition in awe. Consider this your next test for the CEO position. We'll meet back on Monday so you can pitch your ideas to the team."

"Sounds good," Anastasia chirps way too happily for someone who got left out of the dinner last night. "Oh, by the way, the day-care proposal has been approved by legal. We just need Julian's seal of approval since he has the final say in everything." She glances at me and flutters her lashes. "Maybe we can go over it at dinner tonight, so we can move forward?"

I bite back what I want to say—*what the hell are you up to?*—and go with, "Sure, sweetheart. That sounds good."

"Great! See you later." She leans in and kisses my cheek and then stands and practically skips over to the door before turning back around. "Oh, Dad," she says, "lunch today?" This time, when she speaks, her facial expression matches her genuine tone. She's not asking him to lunch as a ploy. She's doing it because she loves her dad and is trying to make shit right.

Samuel grins. "That sounds lovely. I look forward to it."

Once she's gone, Samuel looks at me and says, "We need to talk. IT flagged your IP address last night." He pushes a packet of papers my way. "IT verified several inappropriate sites had been viewed on your work laptop."

"What?" I hiss, flipping through page after page. "That can't be right."

"They confirmed your password had been entered. Have you given anyone else access to your laptop or given them your password?"

"No. I would never give my passwords to anyone." I take my position at Kingston seriously and would never jeopardize it over fucking porn.

"Look," he says, pursing his lips in disappointment, "accessing porn of any kind at work is unacceptable, but I have to say, as your future father-in-law, the fact that you were watching"—he leans and whispers the rest—"gay porn is a bit disconcerting."

What the actual fuck?

"Sir, I—"

And then it hits me. My laptop was in my home office last night while I was at Lush. Anastasia could've easily grabbed my password from where I keep it in my desk drawer and used it.

Motherfucker. I've been set up.

She'd warned me, but I didn't think she'd act this quickly or do something this devious.

"I'm sorry, Samuel," I tell him as I mentally come up with ways to destroy my fiancée. "I don't know what happened, but I'll get to the bottom of it, and it won't happen again."

"Please see to that," he says. "The last thing I want is my daughter getting caught in a scandal. She's been through a lot, and I worry something like that could send her running when I've only just gotten her back."

"I understand."

I stalk straight back to my desk and pull my laptop out of my briefcase, firing it up. I find that my internet history has been wiped clean, which IT can do remotely.

I push out of my seat and go straight for Anastasia's office, finding her typing away at her desk.

"Oh, hey," she says, her tone too fucking upbeat to be sincere. "What's up?"

"Did you do it?" I ask, getting straight to the point. "Did you put goddamn gay porn on my work laptop?" I slam my hands on the top of her desk and lean over it, glaring at her.

"I don't know what you're talking about," she says innocently. "But if that's what you like, maybe this engagement isn't going to work out. I don't exactly have the right equipment ... if you catch my drift."

She smirks, and before I can think, I'm rounding her desk. She sees me coming and gets out of her seat, but before she can get away—or hell, maybe come after me because she's that fucking crazy—I push her against the wall.

With my hips pressed against hers, I slide my knee between her legs and wrap my fingers gently around her throat. I would never hurt a woman, and I'm still fully in control, but, fuck, I'm fuming, and her innocent act is only making it worse.

"This is how you want to play it, Red?" I ask, squeezing her throat just enough to get my point across, but not enough that she's in pain or struggling.

"Damn right it is," she hisses, glaring daggers at me. "Do your worst, *fiancé.*"

I squeeze a little tighter and notice her legs clench around my knee. Of course she's turned on right now.

"You like this, don't you?" I taunt.

"I don't know what you're talking about," she denies, but I've got her number.

"The games," I clarify, then lift my knee slightly, rubbing it across her material-clad cunt. "I bet if I reached into your pants, I'd find you dripping fucking wet."

"You *wouldn't,*" she challenges, telling me she's just as turned on as I am.

Yeah, I'm pissed, but fuck if I'm not turned on. I never expected this woman to be an actual adversary, but she's been shocking me at every turn. Instead of pulling the daughter card, she's fighting for the position with everything she has.

"Is that what you want, Red?" I lean in and snag the tip of her earlobe and bite down, making her groan. "You want me to reach in and, using your juices, make you come right here in your office?"

Her legs tighten around me, and I chuckle.

"Well, that's not gonna happen," I say. "Only good girls get orgasms, baby. And you've been a bad, bad girl."

"Julian," she breathes, letting her hormones get the better of her.

"The next time you do something like that, the only thing you'll be getting is a goddamn spanking."

I release her throat, and she huffs as I step back.

"You want to be treated like *one of the guys*? Fine. But be careful what you wish for."

Without waiting for her to respond, I turn my back on her and head toward her door.

My hand has just landed on the knob when I hear her call out, her voice overly sweet, "Does that mean you don't want to have dinner together tonight?"

"Unless it involves you taking my cock down that throat of yours to make up for what you did, no," I tell her right before I swing the door open and stalk out, slamming it behind me.

"GAY PORN?" RYDER CRACKS UP. "SHE'S GOOD."

"She's playing with fire. I've worked too damn hard to let her destroy my career and reputation."

"Oh, calm down," he says, still laughing. "A little porn action isn't going to get you fired."

"You should've seen the look on Samuel's face, man. He was so disappointed, thinking I was watching gay porn behind his precious daughter's back." I sigh and scrub my hands over my face. "I definitely underestimated her. I mean, gay porn? What the fuck?"

"Maybe you should tell him the truth," Ryder says, sobering. "If he knows it was her ..."

"Fuck that." I sit back in the visitor seat and spread my legs out in front of me. "I'm no snitch."

Ryder barks out a laugh. "You guys are crazy. Maybe after you two destroy each other, I'll go after the CEO position after all."

I glare his way, and he raises his hands in the air.

"Kidding, bro. Chill. I got too much going on anyway."

"Yeah, how's *that* going?" I ask, referring to his fiancée being pregnant.

"Baby is healthy. We got to see him on the ultrasound."

"*Him*?"

"We're not sure yet." He shrugs. "But Nora swears it's a boy … says it's her motherly intuition." He rolls his eyes. "I guess she's rubbed off on me. As much as I want to resent her getting pregnant, I'm excited to be a dad."

"You know you can be a dad without marrying her," I tell him. "Nobody would fault you for walking away from her, and you'd still be a damn good dad."

"I know," he murmurs, "but then what? I'd be an every-other-weekend—"

Before he can finish his sentence, there's a quick knock on the door, followed by the she-devil—Nora, not Anastasia. I know—it's hard to keep track of all the evil women trying to pull us down into hell.

"Generally, when someone knocks, they wait for the other person to grant them access," I say, taking my shitty mood out on her.

Of course, she glares with enough crazy that I wonder if she's casting a spell on me—hell, I wouldn't be surprised if she was a witch. Maybe she and Red both run in the same witch circle.

"Josie said it was only *you* in Ryder's office with him. We're having lunch together."

"And that's my cue to leave."

I glance at Ryder, hitting him with a look that conveys, *Good fucking luck with her*, and then head out of his office, determined to figure out a way to get back at Red.

She wants to make this shit personal? I can do that too. Everyone has skeletons in their closet, and I'm about to find hers. When I'm done with her, she's going to wish she hadn't messed with me. I've worked too hard to get to where I am to let her fuck it all up.

But first, I'm going home to shower, and while I do so, I'll be imagining how damn sexy she looked against the wall with my hand wrapped around her neck while she practically begged me to get her off.

Fuck, I'm so fucked.

"We'll discuss it tomorrow at the meeting. Bring the numbers and—"

My words come to a quick halt as I stare out back at the pool, which is currently occupied by none other than Anastasia. I didn't see her when I got home, and I assumed she was working upstairs since her car was in the garage.

But I was wrong. Way fucking wrong … unless working involves her swimming laps in the pool, topless.

"Julian, you there?" Ryder asks.

"I gotta go."

Without waiting for him to respond, I hang up and pocket my phone, then walk outside. She must hear the French doors close behind me because she glances back and then stops when she reaches the wall.

She turns around to face me, her arms spreading out behind her along the edge. As she lightly kicks her feet out, her body bobs up and down in the water, making her perky tits play peekaboo.

Such a goddamn tease.

"Wasn't expecting you home so early," she says with a smirk.

"Working from home this afternoon."

"Same," she says.

My eyes descend her body, expecting to see bikini bottoms, only there aren't any because she's completely fucking naked.

"Skinny-dipping in the pool, huh?" I say, remembering our conversation when she first moved in. "If you want my attention, you only have to ask."

"Don't flatter yourself. I just don't want any tan lines."

She scowls, clearly not liking the way I threw her past in her face—which gives me an idea.

She drops her arms and dips her face into the water, then pushes off the edge and swims like a fish across to the other side. With the water crystal clear, I can just make out her naked body.

Great. Now, I can add this visual to my spank bank for when I'm getting myself off later.

This woman is seriously going to be the death of me … unless I do something to take her down first.

Sixteen

ANASTASIA

Julian has been quiet. And that scares me.

I expected him to retaliate after the gay-porn incident, but instead, he left work early to work from home—where he found me in the pool, skinny-dipping.

I'd like to say it was a coincidence, but after I heard him tell Josie he was leaving, I hauled ass home. After he had pinned me up against the wall and had me all but begging for release, he'd deserved to be teased right back.

I spent the rest of the afternoon working from under his cabana since it was beautiful out, and when I finally went inside to shower, waiting for me on the kitchen counter was a note.

A bet is a bet. Your home-cooked dinner is in the warmer.

I was a little worried that he'd poisoned it, but I was so hungry, and it smelled so good. I took my chances, and it was delicious.

Yesterday, I learned from Josie that Julian was working from home *again*. And, yes, I'm aware it looks bad that I wasn't even aware of that, which was why I texted him, telling him it would be nice to be kept in the loop so I didn't look like a dumbass in the future.

He thumbs-upped my text, and I wanted to text back where he could shove that damn thumb, but refrained. I spent the day working on my idea, getting to know people in the marketing department and consulting them regarding my thoughts. I learned who was Team Julian and noted ways to win them over.

Once again, when I got home, there was a plate of food waiting for me, just as delicious.

Now, it's Friday morning, and I'm shocked to find that Julian has already left for work. I've been so nervous about him retaliating that it's been hard to concentrate, but seeing as it's been a couple days, I feel like if he was going to strike, he would've already done so.

And that type of thinking is exactly why I'm not expecting what happens next. I walk into the break room at work, pull a mug from the cabinet, and pop a Nespresso pod into the machine. As I inhale the sweet aroma of blonde espresso, my eyes wander to the corkboard, and I almost have a heart attack.

Because pinned to the board is an eight-by-ten collage of scandalous photos from my past. The title, printed in the same font used for Kingston Limited branding reads, *Daddy's Princess Marketing with the Wrong Assets*.

And underneath it is damn near every embarrassing and incriminating photo in color.

I snatch it off the board, looking at every picture—from partying on the beach to experimenting with weed—and I relive the embarrassment and shame all over again. After I got my shit together my sophomore year of college, I put these days behind me. I retook the classes I'd failed, and I graduated with honors.

How Julian got these photos, I have no idea, but he's going to pay for this. I put porn on his laptop, but nobody but my dad and IT knew about it. He hung this on the board for everyone to see.

And then it hits me. Are there any more of these?

I rush out of the break room and straight to Julian's office, barging in without knocking. He's on the phone, but when he sees me, he tells whoever is on the other line that he'll call them back.

"Morning, fiancée, what can I—"

"How dare you!" I hiss, slamming the poster on his desk. "You took this too far!"

"Seriously?" Julian scoffs. "You put fucking porn on my computer, but I went too far?"

"It was a joke!" I shout. "But what you did was personal."

He leans over the desk, his eyes locking with mine. "You don't get it because you were born into this life," he says, his voice low, like he's struggling to contain his anger. "I've had to fight tooth and nail for every ounce of respect I've earned, and your *joke* could've easily destroyed the reputation I've built for myself. Porn on a company device is considered gross misconduct and grounds for immediate termination."

Oh shit. He's right.

"I-I didn't think about that," I say, taken aback by his admission. "I didn't consider the possible consequences."

"Of course you didn't," he hisses. "Why would you? You don't have anything to lose ... not like I do. If you don't get the position, you have an entire trust fund to fall back on. All I have is my reputation. When I started here, I was nothing more than a poor kid from the wrong side of the tracks, but I've spent years busting my ass to become something more. I've earned my position, and I'll be damned if you're going to ruin everything I've worked for."

"I'm sorry," I tell him, meaning it. Yeah, I'm upset about what he did to me, but now that he's laying it all out on the table, I was in the wrong too. "I was pissed, and it was petty," I admit. "But please, I need to know where you put the other posters."

I point at the one on his desk, trying like hell to keep my traitorous tears from falling, but the thought of my dad seeing this and being reminded of what a failure his daughter was has them spilling over.

"If my dad sees them ..." I choke out a sob. "He can't see them. Those pictures are a reminder of every time I messed up, proving why I would never be good enough to run this company. They're of me lashing out because I was craving his attention and he wouldn't look my way.

Only when he did, he told me I didn't deserve to be a Kingston. That he was disappointed and ashamed of me."

I walk around the desk, and he turns his chair so he's facing me.

"Please, nobody else can see those pictures, especially not my dad," I cry, tears sliding down my cheeks. I should probably be embarrassed about Julian seeing me this upset and weak, but I just don't have it in me to care.

Julian shocks me by lifting me into his arms and carrying me over to the couch. He sets me on his lap and wipes my tears.

"Ana," he murmurs, using the name only my mom has ever called me, "I know you think your dad was disappointed and ashamed, and he might've said those words out of anger, but I listened to him talk about you for years, and I swear, he was—and is—so damn proud of you."

"Yet he didn't want me to work for him," I whisper, trying to get ahold of my emotions.

"Did he actually say that, or did you assume it?"

"I was supposed to work for him after graduation, but after my mom died, I was devastated and told him it was best if I left, that I needed to get away from here for a little while. I needed time to grieve. I thought he would ask me to stay, but instead, he agreed and let me go. And not once over the years has he asked me to come back."

Julian nods in understanding. "I'm sorry about the poster, but it's the only one. I hung it up right before you got in, knowing you'd go straight there and see it. I never intended for anyone but you to see it."

"Thank you. And I'm sorry about the gay porn. I would never try to risk your reputation. It was a stupid, thoughtless prank."

"Yeah, well, you got me good," he says with a small smile. "Your dad was not thrilled that his future son-in-law had chosen to watch gay porn on the company laptop."

"Oh God," I groan. "I'll tell my dad what I did."

"It's all good, Red," he says. "But just for the record, the only thing I've been getting off to lately are thoughts of you."

He shifts us slightly, and it's then I realize I'm straddling his lap, and because I'm wearing a pencil skirt, it's ridden up my thighs, making it so my thin panties are rubbing against Julian's groin. We both glance down at the same time, and when he looks up at me, our gazes clashing, the molten desire in his eyes is evident.

"You've been thinking about me?" I breathe, the heat between us so hot that it's damn near stifling.

"All the fucking time," he admits. "And your little skinny-dipping stunt didn't help."

Instinctively, I run my hands up his torso, stopping where his tie rests. With my eyes locked with his, I undo the knot and then unbutton the first few buttons, exposing a spattering of chest hair.

I lean in and press an open-mouthed kiss to the top of his pec, and he releases a soft groan. So, I give him another kiss, this time to his clavicle. He moans again. I shift slightly so I can press a kiss to his neck when there's a knock on his door, followed by someone walking in.

"Oh shit. Sorry!" Dad says, quickly closing the door behind him and effectively ending the moment.

I climb off Julian, and we both take a second to catch our breaths. Technically, nothing happened, yet between his confession and my mouth on his flesh, it feels like the complete opposite.

"I'd better go see what he needs," Julian says, retying his tie as he stands. He walks over to his chair and puts his jacket back on and then glances at me. "I know we're both going for the same position, but I don't want what happened today to happen again. No more dirty play, Red. If I get this position, it will be because I earned it, not because I stepped on you to get there."

"And what if I get it?" I ask, standing.

"Then, I hope you'll keep me around because from what I've seen so far, you'll be an asset to this company, and I look forward to working with you in the future."

My heart swells at his words, at being told for the first time by someone that I'm an asset and not a complete fuckup.

"Now, I need to ask you something," he says, walking over to me and resting his hand on my hip. "Where do we stand?"

I think about his question for a moment. Had my dad not walked in, I'm almost positive I would've had sex with him right here on his couch in his office. I'm attracted to him, and he's made it clear he feels the same way.

But at the end of the day, could we get past one of us getting the CEO position while the other person doesn't? I don't know. What I do know is that I could fall for this man. I've never felt this way before, and that scares the shit out of me.

"We're okay," I say vaguely, hoping he'll take that answer for now.

Of course, he doesn't. "And what does that mean, Ana?"

The shortening of my name causes my stomach to do a flip-flop. My mom was the only one to call me Ana, growing up. My dad hated it, said it sounded plain and that Anastasia sounded professional and important, but she disagreed, saying she loved it because Ana felt softer and more personal. I haven't heard that name since my mom died, and for some reason, when he says it, it sounds intimate. Like he sees beneath the surface, the same way my mom did.

I want to tell him that I want more and to see where things could go between us, but I'm so overwhelmed by my mixture of emotions that I don't know how to word what I want to say.

As if he can sense my inner turmoil, he smiles softly. "Okay," he says. "I get it. You need more time. But just tell me this. Could you see yourself with a man like me?"

"These days, you're the only man I see."

Seventeen

JULIAN

ME

Don't forget, we leave for Hawaii on Thursday.

I PRESS SEND ON THE TEXT AND SHAKE MY HEAD, knowing it's a dumb text to send since our calendars are synced, but it's Saturday, and I haven't seen or heard from Ana all day.

ANA

I know. Our calendars are synced. Why are you really texting me?

I chuckle at her response. The woman never beats around the bush.

ME

I was wondering if you'll be home for dinner.

ANA

Why? You want to cook for me?

ME

Or take you out ... whichever you prefer.

After having Ana grinding on my lap yesterday and seeing that she wants me despite the tough exterior shell she uses to keep herself safe, I've decided to lay all my cards on the table. The woman is everything I want—smart, fierce, independent, and beautiful. Even though the circumstances aren't ideal due to us fighting for the same position, I would be a dumbass not to take advantage of the fact that I have her living with me for the foreseeable future.

ANA

You can cook for me. What time will you be home?

ME

I am home.

ANA

So am I.

Instead of texting her back, I pocket my phone and go in search of her. After checking all the obvious places—including the pool because a part of me is hoping I'll find her skinny-dipping again—I find her sitting in the library, her laptop open and papers strewn about all over the desk. I didn't realize she'd made this room her own space, but I like knowing she's gotten comfortable here.

She doesn't notice me standing in the doorway, so I take a few moments to watch her in her element. Her hair is up in a messy bun, held together by a pen, and her face is clean of makeup, showing off the beautiful spatter of freckles she has across her nose. She's sporting a thin tank top, minus a bra, and because it's chilly in this room, her nipples are on display.

With a pen between her lips and her brows furrowed in concentration, she types furiously, no doubt planning world domination—or a Kingston Limited takeover. The woman is the entire fucking package, and if I have it my way, instead of fighting for power, we'll rule Kingston together. I just need to figure out how to make that happen.

"Maybe you should take a picture," she says without looking up. "Then, you won't have to continue staring at me like a creeper."

I chuckle at her unfiltered words. "I prefer the real deal," I volley. "Pictures don't do you justice."

She glances up and makes a show of rolling her eyes in an attempt to appear unaffected, but the soft pink now tinting her cheeks gives her away.

"What do you want, Parker?" she asks, calling me by my last name, like the guys at work do. She's never done it before, and if I had to guess, it's her veiled attempt at keeping me at a distance.

"I'm bored." I shrug and walk over to where she's working and have a seat across from her. "Whatcha working on?"

"My pitch."

When she doesn't elaborate, I laugh. "You wanna share with the class?"

"Why? So you can undermine it—or better yet, try to steal it?"

It's my turn to roll my eyes. "I'll share my idea with you."

"Go for it." She sits back and crosses her arms over her chest, plumping her perky tits up.

Not wanting to look like a perv for staring, I focus on her face when I say, "He's a musician, so I think we should host a party in Vegas."

"Of course you do," she scoffs.

"In case you forgot, his next club opening is there. We could sponsor the event and have him feature his drink and our liquor. Similar to what the sporting venues we partner with do."

I wait for her to talk more shit, but instead, she stares at me thoughtfully before she says, "Actually ... that's a good idea, and it goes along with my idea."

"I'm sorry." I chuckle. "Did you just say I had a good idea?"

"Don't be annoying." She turns her laptop around so we can both see her screen. "I was thinking we could partner with one of the rideshare companies to promote drinking responsibly and have Ronan be the face of the campaign. He could promote his drink along with the campaign. We could call it something like RideSafe, and Kingston would sponsor it by providing discounted rides for people who shouldn't be driving."

"And we could kick it off at the party in Vegas," I add, the details all coming together in my head. "Not only would it endorse Ronan's partnership with Kingston, but it would also be a great way to promote Kingston's stance on drinking responsibly."

"Exactly." Ana smiles. "Two birds, one stone."

"Hell yeah. Let's do it."

For the next several hours, we work together to sort out all the details until Ana's stomach rumbles, reminding us that we haven't eaten.

"You don't have to cook," she says.

"Nah, I don't mind. But since it's nice out, why don't we grill out on the patio and eat outside?"

"That sounds lovely."

Her phone goes off, and she glances at it. Since I'm sitting next to her, I see it's a text from her dad, asking if we're available to do Sunday brunch tomorrow morning.

"I'm down," I tell her without her having to ask.

She texts her dad back and then looks up at me. Our faces are so close that all it would take is us leaning in slightly and our mouths would touch.

Ana licks her lips, her eyes landing on mine, and I slowly release a breath, wondering if I should make a move. It's crazy since we've kissed before, but so much has happened since then. When she sucks in her bottom lip and glances up at me through her lashes, I take that as my sign.

Sliding my arm around the back of the couch we decided to work on earlier, I lean in, my eyes not leaving hers while I give her a chance to push me away or tell me no.

When she does neither, I bridge the rest of the gap between us and press my lips to hers. They feel exactly how I remember—soft and supple—and when she parts them on a sigh, giving me permission to deepen the kiss by sliding my tongue into her mouth, she tastes just as sweet as she did the last time I kissed her.

Unlike our previous kisses that were motivated by our chemistry and passion, this one is slower, gentler. Neither of us is in a rush to take things any further. As we get lost in the kiss, our tongues caressing each other, it's like time has stopped, the world has momentarily disappeared, and all that's left is Ana and me and the way our lips curl so damn perfectly around one another.

And not for the first time, my mind wanders to thoughts of a future with this woman, and unlike with any other woman I've been with, I can see it. Working together to bring Kingston to the next level. Evenings spent talking business over dinner, which lead to heated nights in bed. Sunday brunches, weekends away, introducing her to my family ...

But my thoughts don't stop there. Instead, they continue further—to her wearing my ring and taking my name, turning this house into a home as we fill it with little versions of us ...

Her stomach growls loudly, ending the moment, and we pull back, both of us slightly out of breath.

"Let's get you fed," I tell her, backing up so I can meet her eyes.

"Okay," she says, "but afterward, we should continue where we left off."

When I raise a brow, a bit shocked by her forwardness, she shakes her head.

"I was talking about the pitch." She pushes off my chest and climbs off the couch, stumbling toward the door like she's drunk from our kiss. "Let's go, Parker," she yells behind her. "I'm starved."

Jesus, after that kiss, I am too. But it's sure as hell not for food.

"I FORGOT HOW BEAUTIFUL THE BEACHES IN MAUI are." Ana sighs in awe as she takes in the view of the sunset on our balcony while the only view I'm interested in is her.

Her hair is up in a tight ponytail, showing off her slim neck, which I want to kiss every inch of. She's wearing a strapless white floral minidress with a pink-flowered lei she received when we arrived hanging around her neck. She looks beautiful, and the only thing I want to do this week is get lost in her—even if we are here for Ryder's wedding.

After dinner, despite my best efforts, nothing else happened between Ana and me. At brunch on Sunday, we ended up pitching our idea to Samuel when it got brought up, and from there, everything went into overdrive.

We spoke with Ronan, and after he agreed to the collaboration—and his agent gave the green light—we moved forward full force.

The event is taking place in less than a month, and with us being here for this absurd wedding, that leaves us less than three weeks to handle all the arrangements.

The team back home is working on it, but Ana is hands-on, like I am, so we've been buried neck deep in the details.

The three days before we got here, we worked damn near around the clock, not having a moment to ourselves. And when we got home, both of us were too tired to even think about taking things further—okay, obviously I thought about it, but I was too exhausted to do anything about it.

Our eight-hour flight here was spent with us catching up on our sleep, and now, I'm awake and ready to see where things can go between us. I just have to hope she's on the same page.

"We have the day to ourselves," I tell her, resting my hands on the railing and caging her in from behind. "What do you say we get some brunch down by the pool and spend the day relaxing? I booked us a private cabana." I lean down and give her heated flesh a kiss, making her shiver in response.

"I'd say that sounds like heaven." She turns slightly, and her eyes home in on my lips.

With her gaze filled with lust, I assume she's going to kiss me, but instead, she ducks under my arm and steps back inside.

"I'm going to get my suit on," she says, leaving me standing on the balcony alone and wondering if maybe she regrets our kiss the other night and isn't interested in anything more happening between us.

A few minutes later, she comes out of the bathroom, sporting a tiny black bikini with gold hoops on each of her hips and one in the middle of her breasts, holding the fabric together. The swells of her breasts are on display, along with her toned stomach, and when she walks past me, the bottoms of her ass cheeks are peeking out. The bathing suit covers a lot more than the one she wore the day on the boat—probably because her family and coworkers are here—but it still shows off her gorgeous body.

"I'm ready," she says after throwing her see-through cover-up on.

Her gaze slides down my body, checking me out—I changed into my boardshorts while she was changing and haven't put on my shirt yet—and with the way her hazel eyes darken with lust, I'm about to change our plans and not leave this room until I've fucked her any way she'll let me—at least two times.

But when she slips on her flip-flops and saunters to the door, I snap out of it, snatch my shirt off the bed, and follow after her like a damn puppy.

"Do you think we could get my dad on board with moving the company headquarters to Maui?"

We've been switching back and forth between the beach and the pool all afternoon, and now, we're lying on lounge chairs under a large canopy on the beach, only a few feet away from the water. Anastasia's using her elbows to prop herself up, and in doing so, her breasts are jutted out. She's slick from the oil she used earlier, and the thought of sliding my cock between her tits is stuck in my head.

"Huh?" I ask, knowing she asked something, but for the life of me, I can't remember what.

She rolls her eyes and shakes her head and is about to give me shit when Ryder comes running over.

"Hey! A bunch of us are going to play volleyball. Wanna play?"

"Sure," I say. I haven't done any form of exercise today, so it'll be good to get a workout in. "Hey, babe. Wanna watch your man kick ass in volleyball?"

I waggle my brows playfully, and she scrunches up her nose in disgust.

"Seriously? Because I'm a woman, it's assumed I'm sitting on the sidelines while you play?"

Ryder cracks up laughing.

"Definitely not," he tells her. "If you wanna play, you're more than welcome to."

"Great." She slides off the chair. "I want to be on whatever team Julian's not on, so he can watch as I kick *his ass* in volleyball."

With a dramatic wink, she runs off toward the net, leaving Ryder laughing.

"She's something else," he says, his eyes not leaving her.

"And she's mine, so keep your eyes to yourself."

Ryder chuckles. "Just appreciating the view."

"Maybe if you were marrying someone you actually wanted to marry, you'd be too busy appreciating *her* view to notice my fiancée."

"Your fake fiancée," he points out, deflecting.

"Semantics." I side-eye him. "My point is, it's not too late to call the wedding off."

"Not happening," he says. "And speaking of weddings—or in your case, *non*-weddings"—he smirks—"when this whole charade is over, what will you do with all the time you'll have with her not busting your balls?"

"I still have a while to figure that out. You, on the other hand, have less than forty-eight hours until you marry a woman you don't want to spend your life with."

"I'm not calling anything off, so drop it," he says in a tone that brooks no argument.

"Please tell me you at least made her sign a prenup."

"Of course," he scoffs. "I'm not a complete idiot." He smacks my chest and takes off running. "Let's go, Parker! Your woman and I need to kick your ass!"

"You're teaming up with her?" I call back, chasing after him. "What happened to bros over hos?"

"Sorry, man." Ryder laughs. "I've heard the shit she's done. I'm not getting on her bad side."

Eighteen

ANASTASIA

Today should've been relaxing. We're on the beach of an all-inclusive resort in Maui. All I have to do is raise a finger, and another drink is put in my hand. Work is temporarily on hold. Between the cabana by the pool and the lounge chairs with the canopy on the beach, Julian has made sure we're comfortable and relaxed.

But I'm not relaxed … because all day, I've had to look at a half-naked Julian. When he swims and walks and bends over, his corded muscles contract in a way that shouldn't be sexy, but is. And those tattoos. I'd like to say I forgot he had them on his chest since it'd been a while since I'd seen him shirtless, but the truth is, they've been in several of my fantasies over the past few weeks. It's a bit easier to ignore how gorgeous the man is when he's dressed in a suit, covering all of his goods. But the second his shirt came off, I was a goner.

I forgot how built he was despite us being on the boat not that long ago. So much has happened since then. Yet, with all that's happened, it's clear I'm still attracted to Julian. Only now, it's worse because I've gotten to know him. So, instead of only being turned on by his looks, I'm equally falling for his personality.

The way he constantly makes sure I'm taken care of. If my drink is close to being empty, he's on it. If my skin is showing too much pink, he's applying sunscreen on me.

And I'd like to say it's the island. We're on vacation, and I'm living in a fantasy bubble. But it started before we came here. When our pranks got out of hand and I cried, he held me. He apologized and meant it. He didn't have to tell me how proud my dad was of me, but he did.

He cooks me dinner every night. And ever since he realized I use the library as my office, he had a better light put in, along with an air filter since it smelled a bit like old books.

Right now, I'm standing on the other side of the net, watching as Julian bends over, his tanned skin glistening with a mixture of sunscreen and sweat, ready for the volleyball to come his way. And all I can think about it is whether he sweats like that in bed. If he's capable of going long enough and hard enough to work up a sweat like that. I imagine him hovered above me, thrusting in and out of me as I run my fingertips along his sweaty back, digging my nails into his heated flesh.

Jesus, I can't remember the last time I was this turned on. I release a harsh breath and wonder if anyone would notice if I disappeared to our room to rub one out really quick.

Just as the thought enters my brain, the ball goes over the net, and Julian pops up, ready to make the return. His arms stretch out in front of him, and as he makes contact, his muscles contract, making the apex of my legs do the same.

He spikes the ball over the net, and before anyone on our side can get to it, it hits the sand, giving them the point they need to win the game.

"Hell yeah!" Julian yells, pointing at me and grinning as he runs over to me. "Just call me Master, baby, because I'm the master of damn near everything."

"Congratulations, *Master*," I say dryly, patting his hard, glistening chest. "Now, how about you go be the master of cleaning up our stuff that we left over by our chairs so I can head up to our room and start getting ready for dinner?"

My dad texted earlier and asked us to go on a double date with him and Selene since he hasn't seen us all day. With them being a bit older, they chose to relax indoors and booked a couples spa day.

"Yeah, yeah." Julian chuckles. "I'll meet you upstairs."

With a kiss to my cheek, he takes off toward our chairs, and I head in the opposite direction with the hope of getting to our room with enough time to give myself some sexual relief.

Since I'm full of sand from playing volleyball, I grab my waterproof vibrator and take it with me into the bathroom. I turn the water on hot and leave my suit on so I can rinse it off.

After rinsing the sand off me, I remove my bikini bottoms and top and hang them on the hook to dry out.

Lifting one leg onto the shower bench, I push the vibrator inside me with one hand while pinching my nipple with the other. The vibration instantly hits me in all the right places, and I close my eyes, more than ready to get some relief.

Usually, if I want to get off, I either turn to a steamy page in one of my favorite romance books, or if I'm lazy, I check out some porn that I'd never admit to watching. But with Julian fresh in my mind, as I stand under the spray with my vibrator doing its job, I don't need anything but the visual of him to get me off.

"How about you let me help you with that?" a masculine voice says.

At first, I think it's my mind playing tricks on me ... imagining Julian's sexy voice while I get off to the images of him today. Only a second later, when his front presses against my back and his hand wraps around my hand that's holding the vibrator, I realize I'm not imagining his voice and he's actually in the shower with me.

My eyes shoot open, and I glance back at him.

"What are you doing?" I whisper, too turned on to be embarrassed over getting caught with a sex toy between my legs. A woman has needs ...

"What I want to know is why you're using this"— with his hand wrapped around mine, he pulls the vibrator out, and my body immediately weeps at the loss—"when you have me at your disposal."

He turns me around and presses me up against the wall, and it's then I notice he's still in his board shorts.

"Because unlike you, my vibrator doesn't come with any strings or complications."

He nods, knowing I'm not wrong. Every time we get too close, my brain malfunctions, and my pussy does all the thinking. But the second I'm away from Julian, my brain remembers what my pussy refuses to acknowledge—getting involved with him would be stupid on many levels. And I pride myself on being smart.

"Okay," he says, leaning in and nipping at my bottom lip. "Then, let's keep it uncomplicated."

I should note that he doesn't say stringless, but I'm too busy thinking with my pussy because as he finishes his sentence, he punctuates it by sucking my bottom lip into his mouth.

As I lean against the cool wall, he lets go of my lip and then trails kisses along my jaw and over to my ear. "Can I make you come, Red?" he whispers against the shell of my ear.

And just like that, my brain has left the building, leaving my pussy to do all the thinking. And of course, that slut is all about coming.

I nod my answer, but that's not good enough for Julian.

"I need to hear the words," he murmurs in between sucking on my heated flesh. "Tell me you want me to pin you against this wall and shove my cock so deep inside you that you don't know where I end and you begin." He kisses and sucks on my clavicle. "Tell me you want me to fuck you so good that you come all over my goddamn cock."

"What about my vibrator?" I squeak out, his dirty talk turning me on.

"This?" He lifts it up to my lips and presses the power button. "Open."

I do as he said, and he pushes it into my mouth.

"Close and suck."

My lips wrap around the vibrating rubber, and his eyes heat in desire.

"Good girl. Have you ever taken a cock in your ass?"

Oh God. I squirm at the thought. I love anal play. It doesn't happen often because I need to be with someone long enough to be that intimate with them, and my goal in life has been to not let anyone get too close, but I'm no stranger to using butt plugs and dildos in my ass myself occasionally. Again, a woman has needs.

Because I have a vibrating dildo in my mouth, I nod enthusiastically, and Julian's eyes light up.

"You like it in the ass, baby?" he confirms.

Another quick nod.

He pulls the dildo out and spins me around, pushing my back until I fold over so my ass is on display. He gives it a good squeeze and then pushes a couple of digits into my pussy.

"Fuck, you're dripping wet." He finger-fucks me without holding back, and when I'm close to coming, he pulls his fingers out, leaving me hanging.

I whine at the loss—*again*—but it's short-lived because a moment later, his fingers push into my ass, making me moan in pleasure. I didn't think about the logistics of anal in the shower, but thankfully, Julian did, using my juices as lube. He works my ass over for several minutes before he pulls his fingers out and replaces them with the vibrating rubber dick. The overwhelming sensation damn near sends me over the edge.

With it vibrating in my ass, Julian grabs the curves of my hips and murmurs, "Hold on, Red. I'm about to fuck you into next week."

And then, giving me only enough time to press my hands on the wall so I'm not shoved into it, he thrusts into me from behind.

His cock is thick, and mixed with the dildo in my ass, it's a tight squeeze. But because I'm so turned on, he moves in and out of me easily, fucking me just how he promised. Over and over, his thick length hits all the right spots, and within minutes, my pussy is contracting around his cock as I climax harder than I ever have in my life.

"Fuck," he groans, digging his fingers into my flesh as he drains his orgasm into me.

We both stay where we are, catching our breaths, and then the vibrator is turned off and slowly removed out of my ass, followed by Julian pulling out of me. The double loss causes a shiver from the cold to overcome me despite the shower being hot and steamy.

As if Julian can sense what I'm feeling, he pulls me into a standing position and wraps his arms around me from behind, instantly warming my body up.

Wordlessly, he goes about washing my hair and then my body. When he gets to the area between my legs, he turns me around and says, "Lift your leg."

I place it on the bench, and then he swipes a washcloth between my legs. I'm sensitive, and I wince, and he smirks knowingly. He warned me he would fuck me into next week, and he wasn't lying. Even sensitive and a bit sore from the double penetration, I'm already thinking about when I can have him again.

"Are you on birth control?" he asks, tapping my leg so I can put it down.

"Huh?"

I'm so lost in the clouds that I don't realize what he's asking until he clarifies, "Birth control. I came inside you."

"Oh." Jesus, I've never had unprotected sex. "Yeah, I have an IUD. We're protected."

"Good," he says. "Wouldn't want to knock you up before convincing you to take my name."

I wait for him to laugh or say he's joking, but he doesn't. Since I'm sure he's just messing with me, I let it go, focusing on the other part of having unprotected sex.

"I'm clean. I haven't had sex in a while, and I've been tested since then."

"Same," he says, reaching to grab his board shorts—which he shucked off at some point—from the floor and hanging them on the hook next to my bikini.

"And now that I've had you raw," he says, leaning in and nipping my lip, "there's no way in hell I'm fucking you with a piece of rubber between us."

Without giving me a chance to respond, he reaches around and fists the back of my hair, pulling my face toward his for a passionate kiss that sets my body on fire and has me wanting round two.

"Not now," he murmurs against my lips. "We have a dinner to get to. And the next time I take you, I'm going to take my time and explore every inch of you."

Nineteen

JULIAN

WHEN I WALKED INTO THE BATHROOM TO GO PEE, I didn't plan on having sex with Ana, let alone hot fucking shower sex that involved her vibrating pink rubber dildo. But I can't say I regret it in the least because it was the best sex of my life. And that says a lot because I've had my fair share of sex.

I wasn't sure which woman I'd get—the proper marketing analyst who prefers luncheons over clubs or the feisty woman who deflated my tires and put gay porn on my laptop. Based on the way her eyes lit up at the idea of anal and how she screamed while she came all over my cock, feisty Ana was who I was fucking. And, holy shit, do I want more.

After we finished showering and drying off, I left her to get ready while I got dressed. We're attending a luau with her dad and Selene, so I'm dressed in a pair of gray linen pants, a long-sleeved white button-down, rolled to my elbows, and a pair of flip-flops.

I'm returning an email when Ana steps out of the bathroom, dressed in a low-cut, long tropical dress that shows off the swells of her breasts with a slit that runs straight up her thigh, exposing her toned, tanned leg. Her hair is down in perfect waves, and she put on a fresh face of makeup, complete with her signature bright red lipstick that matches the color of the flowers on her dress. She saunters over to where a pair of heels are waiting for her and slides them on.

"Do I look like I belong here?" she asks, doing a playful twirl.

"You look like you belong riding my cock," I say, standing and walking over to her. I grip the curve of her hip with one hand and run my other up her smooth thigh and around to her backside, learning that she's only wearing a tiny piece of fabric that I'd bet barely covers her cunt and nothing more.

"Please tell me you don't mind giving head because the thought of you wrapping those lips around my shaft and staining it red might sound cliché, but it's got me sporting a semi."

Ana throws her head back with a melodic laugh, and like opposite poles of a magnet, I'm drawn to the column of her neck, peppering kisses along it while inhaling her signature floral scent that, tonight, is mixed with coconut from her suntan lotion she was reapplying all day.

"Oh God," she mutters, shaking her head. "If you keep doing that, we'll never make it out of this room." She backs up slightly and locks eyes with me. "But for the record, I love giving head, and if you play your cards right, by the end of the night, my lips will be wrapped around your dick."

With a playful wink, she walks past me, stopping to brush her fingertips along my groin. I grab her hand and tug her toward me, but it doesn't take much since she comes willingly.

Reaching up, she whispers, "And if you're a good boy, I'll even let you fuck my mouth. A little fun fact: I have no gag reflex."

"That's it!" I lift her over my shoulder, and she shrieks in shock. "The only place we're going to is the bedroom." I give her ass a hard slap, making her giggle.

"Julian, put me down!" she yells through her laughter as she pounds my back. "We have to go to dinner, and you're messing up my hair."

"Oh, baby," I tell her, setting her down on her feet since she's right. As much as I want nothing more than to rip our clothes off and sink into her, we can't stand her dad and Selene up.

"We need to take pictures before dinner," I say, grabbing my wallet, phone, and room key. "Because afterward, I'm going to be messing up a whole lot more than your hair."

"Mmm," she moans dramatically. "I can't wait."

With another smack to her ass—this one not as hard—I push her out the door before we don't make it to dinner.

When we arrive at the luau, we show the hostess our IDs, and we're each given a wristband, indicating we're old enough to drink. Then, a woman places a bright pink-and-white-flowered lei over each of our heads.

We thank her and then stop at the drink station, each grabbing a mai tai before we make our way over to the table where Ana's dad and Selene are sitting with a drink in their hands.

"Mmm," Ana moans, taking a sip. "Delicious."

I take a sip of mine and have to agree. It's a good quality drink.

"Oh, Anastasia. You look beautiful," Selene gushes when she spots us. "Hawaii definitely agrees with you."

She envelops Ana in a motherly embrace. I'm not sure if it's because of the sun she's gotten today or if she's overwhelmed by the affection, but when she thanks Selene, she says it almost shyly, her cheeks tinted a light shade of pink that I didn't notice before. Then, Samuel stands to give her a hug as well.

We've spoken about her strained relationship with her dad, but she hasn't said anything about how she feels with him being married. I know she was close with her mom, so I imagine it's hard to see him with someone else. And because Selene is literally the nicest person, it's impossible to hate her.

We have a seat across from her dad and Selene, and I drape my arm across Ana's shoulders. I'm not sure how she'll react since we're no longer in the heat of passion, so I'm shocked when she snuggles against me and rests her head on my chest, letting me hold her.

The music dies down, and the DJ announces that the show is about to begin, so we turn our attention to the stage. It's dark outside, but the lights around the area and on the stage create a glow to showcase the dancers. The music kicks on, and they start dancing.

The performance is entertaining, and at one point, they convince Ana to go onstage and join them. She shakes her hips like a pro, and I can't take my eyes off of her.

When the show ends and everyone claps, they encourage us all to get up and dance.

"Dance with me," Ana asks, tugging on my hand.

"I'm nowhere near drunk enough to embarrass myself like that," I say with a laugh.

"Please." She pouts, showing me a new side of her— the cute, playful side.

"Not happening. I'd rather watch you."

Her pout deepens, and then she leans in and whispers, "I wonder how my lipstick will look on your cock," knowing damn well she's got me.

"You play hardball, Red," I groan, standing and taking her hand in mine.

A beautiful smile spreads across her face, and I can't help staring at her.

"What?" she asks. "Why are you looking at me like that?"

"You look different," I tell her, pulling her into my arms and swaying to the music.

"Different how?" she questions, her brows furrowing in confusion.

"You look happy. Watching you genuinely laugh and smile all day has made me realize how much you tamp down your emotions on a regular basis. Or maybe you haven't had a reason since you arrived in Rosemary to laugh and smile like you do here."

I cup the side of her face, and she sighs into my hand.

"Regardless," I tell her, dipping my head so our mouths are only centimeters apart, "I've decided that my new goal in life is to make you laugh and smile like that every day."

Without waiting for her to respond, I kiss her softly, making no move to deepen it. With her in my arms, I'm perfectly content with our bodies and mouths simply being connected.

When they announce dinner will be served soon, we have a seat. Ana stays cuddled into my side, and when Samuel notices, he smiles at me and then at his daughter.

"Selene is right. Hawaii looks good on you both," he says with a grin. "Did you have a good day?"

"We did," Ana says. "I love it here. We spent the day going back and forth between the pool and the beach. I'm not sure which one is more beautiful, but I'm just glad I don't have to choose. We had lunch at Ocean 101, and it was so delicious," she gushes, making her dad and Selene both smile. "You guys should try it." She glances up at me. "I don't know what we're doing tomorrow, but maybe we can meet for lunch there."

"We have plans in the morning, but we can do lunch." I kiss the crown of her head, and she sighs back into me.

"You guys look relaxed as well," I say to Samuel and Selene. "Did you enjoy your spa day?"

Ana doesn't know it, but I have a couples massage scheduled for us tomorrow. She mentioned wanting to get one earlier, so I booked it from my phone.

"We did," Selene answers. "Tomorrow, we might brave the pool for a little bit. Right, Samuel?"

"Maybe," he says, smiling at her. "But I much prefer the time we spend indoors."

He shoots her a wink, and Ana glances at me, her eyes going wide.

"They're like that all the time," I whisper so they can't hear. "Like a couple of horny teenagers. You'll get used to it."

She snorts out a laugh and shakes her head. "I'd rather not."

"I THINK THEY'RE CLOSING DOWN."

Ana glances around for the first time in hours, as if just realizing we're one of the few couples left. Since dinner ended and everyone was encouraged to join the dancers, we've been dancing and drinking. Her dad and

Selene took off a while ago with the promise of meeting us tomorrow for lunch.

"They are," I agree, making no move to leave. Leaving means letting go of Ana, and I'm perfectly content, having her in my arms. "We should probably let them clean up."

She nods in agreement, then takes a step back, swaying slightly due to the many mai tais she consumed. She laughs at herself as I catch her from falling over.

"It's a long walk back." She pouts. "I don't know if I can walk that far."

I chuckle at how adorable a drunk Ana is. "Hop on, my drunk little hula dancer."

I turn around, indicating for her to get on my back, and she cheers in excitement, hopping right on.

"This is definitely earning you a blow job when we get back," she says loud enough for a couple walking by to hear.

Thankfully, they're not prudes, and the girl laughs while the guy grins in understanding.

"The only thing you'll be doing when we get back is passing out."

Sure enough, by the time we get back to the room, Ana's eyes are half-lidded. I lay her on the bed and take her heels off.

"I'm too tired to get changed," she mutters. "Can you help me?"

She lifts her arms, and I laugh again at how cute she is. There are so many sides to Ana, and I love learning about each one. I'm not even done sliding her dress off and putting one of my shirts on her since I can't find her pajamas before she's passed out. I grab her a bottle of water and a pain reliever and set them on her nightstand for the morning, in case she's the type of person to wake up with a headache the morning after drinking.

I change into a pair of sweats, going shirtless since that's how I sleep, and then slide into bed next to her. She turns around, cuddles into my side, and sighs in contentment. And for the first time, I'm completely okay with sleeping with a woman. That should probably scare me, but I've already accepted the fact that I've fallen for Ana, and I have every intention of making her mine.

Now, I just have to get her on board.

NAILS GLIDING DOWN MY SKIN.

Lips kissing my flesh.

My first thought is that this is the beginning of a damn good dream—until I hear my name being called, and I snap my eyes open, finding Ana on her knees, between my legs.

"Please tell me I'm not dreaming," I half joke, making her smile.

"Oh, no, you're awake and about to get the best head of your life."

Fuck yes.

"Do you want to know why?" she asks, rubbing a nail down my torso and through my happy trail, stopping right above the waistline of my sweats.

"Sure," I say, going along with whatever she's doing. Hey, if I know what I did to earn me a morning blow job, I can make sure to do it again, right?

"You danced with me." She plants a kiss to the top of my six-pack, which has me tightening my ab muscles. "You carried me back to the room." Another kiss to just above my navel. "You undressed me." She kisses the spot above my waistline. "And then you not only dressed me in your shirt, but you also left me pain reliever by the bed." She kisses the material right where my cock is, waking it up. "Your gentlemanly behavior has earned you a reward."

"Baby," I say, sitting up slightly and tipping her chin up to look at me, "I don't know what men you've been with, but everything you just said is the bare fucking minimum. I'll take that blow job, but nothing I did earned me one."

I release her chin, and she stares at me for several seconds before she nods in understanding.

"May I?" she asks, wanting my permission to pull my pants off.

"You never need permission to touch me. I don't give a shit if I'm awake, asleep, or, hell, dead for that matter. You want to touch me? Go for it."

She snorts at the last part, then makes a show of pulling my sweats down and exposing my already-halfway-to-hard cock. Even he gives her permission to touch him anytime.

She licks her lips, and it's then I notice she has on a fresh coat of her signature red lipstick. Fuck me. I swear I fall in love with her in this moment. Not only did she wake me up to give me a blow job, but she also reapplied her lipstick first to fulfill a fantasy of mine.

With my sweats off, she wraps her fingers around my shaft and presses a soft kiss to the head. The light touch of her lips has it twitching slightly in excitement.

She gives it another kiss, and when a drop of pre-cum seeps out, she laps it up. Her eyes meet mine, and without looking away, she slowly slides her mouth down my entire shaft, not stopping until I can feel the crown of my cock hitting the back of her throat. Her beautiful hazel eyes water slightly, but she wasn't lying when she said she had no gag reflex.

And then she takes a deep breath and takes me straight down her fucking throat, and it takes all the restraint I have not to blow my load.

She stays like that for several seconds, damn near choking on my cock before she releases it so she can take a breath. Without waiting long, she takes me back down her throat, this time slowly moving up and down.

Her saliva creates the best friction, and despite not wanting this to end, it won't be long until I'm coming. Her mouth feels like heaven personified, and I refuse to think about all the guys she's had those plump lips wrapped around to perfect her technique. But one thing's for sure: my cock is going to be the last cock she ever has those lips wrapped around, if I have any say in the matter.

After I come down her throat and she swallows it like a pro, she sits back and smiles, admiring her red lipstick all over my cock.

"Best work of art I've seen in a while."

She winks playfully, and I sit up, grab her, and flip her onto her back, then kiss her hard for several seconds before I go about removing her clothes.

"Are you comfortable?" I ask, glancing down at her naked body. "Because I meant what I said. I'm going to explore every inch of you, and it's going to take a while."

A slow smile spreads across her face. "Explore away," she says. "My body is yours to do with as you please."

Twenty

ANASTASIA

"As much as I love the multiple orgasms and room service, I feel like we've barely seen Maui," I say as we step outside, and the bright sun hits me hard, forcing me to momentarily close my eyes.

Julian and I have been holed up in our room all day—even going as far as to cancel our lunch plans with my dad and Selene—only coming out because Julian is the best man in the wedding and has to attend the rehearsal and dinner.

"We had a couples massage scheduled," he admits, "but I chose to just massage you myself."

He waggles his brows, and I laugh at his playfulness.

"It's actually been rescheduled for Sunday. And I have an entire day planned, so don't worry. After this ridiculous wedding is done, we'll see plenty of the island before we leave."

He envelops my hand in his and kisses my temple, then guides us toward where the rehearsal is taking place.

"Why are you so against Ryder getting married?" I ask. "Or are you against marriage in general?" I vaguely recall him mentioning something about not wanting to get married when we first met.

"I'm not anti-marriage," he says as we walk down the sidewalk. "My mom and Frank have been happily married for over twenty-five years. They give me shit all the time because I haven't settled down, but the truth is, I always thought I'd be married with kids by now. I just got so wrapped up in work, and the women I met weren't exactly wife material."

"Which is why you went in search of me." I bat my lashes flirtatiously, and he chuckles.

"Actually," he says with a smirk, "I was in search of a woman who could play the part of the submissive, doting wife, but I got you instead." He stops and peers down at me, his smirk now replaced with a look of seriousness. "I never planned for you, Red, but I'm so damn glad I got you."

His admission causes a lump of emotion to clog my throat, making it hard for me to breathe. I wasn't expecting him either, but now, I can't imagine not having him in my life. And that scares the hell out of me because no matter how sizzling the chemistry is between us, how life-altering the sex is, or the way he's recently proven that he makes me laugh and smile, we can never be anything more, and I need to remember that.

He might've mentioned wanting more, but that's only because he's thinking with his dick. Men like Julian don't want women like me long-term, no matter what they say. He said it himself—he was looking for a submissive wife, not one who would give him a run for his money. And it might be fun now, but eventually, he'll get sick of the games.

"There you are!" Ryder comes over and pats Julian on the shoulder, providing a welcome interruption in our conversation.

"Shouldn't you be at the rehearsal?" Julian says with a laugh.

"Forgot my tie," he says with an eye roll. "Nora sent me back to grab it. Can't have me looking like she picked me up off the streets." His phone pings, and he checks it, then groans. "Better get back there. See you in a few."

He takes off running down the sidewalk, and I give Julian a look that says, *What the fuck?*

"If I tell you something, you have to keep it between us."

"Always," I tell him.

"She's pregnant."

"Oh. Is that a bad thing?" I ask, assuming it's not good by his ominous tone.

"She trapped him," he says with disgust. "She said she was on birth control, but Ryder doesn't believe her. He wanted to do the right thing, so he proposed, but shortly after, she miscarried, and I guess she sank into a depression. He felt bad, so he held off on calling off the engagement. And just before he was finally about to do it, his dumbass got drunk one night and gave in to having sex with her. She swore she was on birth control—*again*—and he says he used protection, but a few weeks later, she told him she was pregnant."

"Ouch. That's rough."

"Yeah," he agrees. "He thinks he needs to marry her so he can provide the baby with a loving home. I tried to convince him otherwise, but he won't listen, so as his best friend, I'm going to support him … and when shit comes crashing down—because we all know it will—I'll have his back."

"You're a good friend," I tell him. "And don't worry. I am actually on birth control, one that's good for the next three years, so I won't be trapping you." I wink playfully, and he chuckles.

"I don't know," he says, pulling me into his arms. "The thought of a little hazel-eyed boy or girl running around doesn't sound half bad."

"It's the sun," I deadpan. "It's getting to your brain and frying it."

He barks out a laugh. "Maybe." He backs up and lifts my hand that's intertwined with his, giving it a kiss. "You ready? I have a feeling this rehearsal, dinner, and wedding will be nothing if not entertaining."

"Red, baby, you gotta wake up."

I pry my eyes open and find Julian staring down at me.

"There she is." He smiles and then dips down, giving me a soft kiss. "I need you to get up. It's early, but there's somewhere I want to take you before we have to go to the airport."

I pout at the reminder of us leaving today.

"I know," he says, as if reading my mind. "But I promise we'll be back, and we can stay however long you want."

He presses his lips to mine, and I wrap my legs around him, lifting my pelvis to grind against his groin.

"Not happening, beautiful. Then, we'll never leave, and we have to go now, or we'll miss it."

"Miss what?" I lift my leg so I can roll onto my stomach and hide my face in my pillow.

"It's a surprise. Now, up!"

He smacks my ass, and I jump off the bed, glaring back as I head to the bathroom to get ready, noting that it's still freaking dark outside.

"Dress in warm clothes and comfortable shoes," he adds.

As I sit on the toilet, I think back to how amazing our trip has been despite having to attend the weirdest wedding I've ever been to.

The rehearsal, dinner, and wedding were in fact entertaining, as Julian had predicted. But not in a funny sort of way. It was like watching a horror show. Nora screamed and screeched and whined and sometimes cried. She demanded perfection, and everyone around her scrambled around, afraid of being stomped on by the evil bridezilla, while Ryder looked like he wanted to be anywhere but there.

On a positive note, the wedding venue was beyond beautiful and magical, and even though I've rarely thought about getting married, if I were to, I would want it to be like that wedding—minus the scowling bride, subdued groom, scared employees, and concerned guests.

Not that there were many guests. Aside from Ryder's family—who I learned from Julian is one of the wealthiest families in Texas—there was Nora's family, who were ... fun, to put it nicely. Then, there were Ryder's friends and colleagues and a couple of Nora's mean girlfriends.

Julian and I had a good time though. We danced and drank and ate delicious food. And in between the dinner and wedding, we spent all our spare time getting lost in each other.

Yesterday, we spent the day sightseeing, visiting all the cool places and eating our weight in delicious Hawaiian delicacies. We had a wonderful dinner with my dad and Selene, and we ended the night with Julian fucking me from behind on our balcony as the sun set.

It feels like we've been living in a paradise bubble, and I'm dreading returning to reality, wishing we could stay here forever—which is weird since I'm a workaholic and I've never spent this much time off work or on vacation with someone. It probably has something to do with the dozens of orgasms Julian has given me.

I'm blaming it on the large amounts of oxytocin and dopamine that have been released from my brain. And refusing to acknowledge the fact that I'm falling for Julian ... hard.

The drive to where we're going is long, and he forces me to drink a lot of water since we're heading up high, but the trip is filled with Julian and me taking turns playing twenty questions, so it goes quick. He starts off asking random questions, like what my favorite color and food are. Then, he moves on to ones that require a bit more thinking, like where I would go if I could travel anywhere. And just before we arrive, he squeezes in a few deep questions, like if I see myself having kids one day.

Telling him that I love the color red and would kill for a good Hawaiian pizza was simple. Admitting that I would love to travel to Australia to see the huge spiders and kangaroos people talk about on social media was easy. But having to tell him that I'm afraid to have a family of my own was hard. So, instead, I deflected by saying I could barely keep a plant alive, let alone an entire human. We both laughed it off, but I didn't ask him the same question, instead asking him something lighter.

When we arrive at the Haleakalā National Park gates, Julian pays, and we drive through. The drive continues as we ascend until we reach the summit parking.

"Put these on," he says, handing me a hoodie and a beanie. I'm confused as to why until we get out and I see how chilly it is up here.

"We're ten thousand feet up," he says, grabbing something from the trunk of the rental.

When I look closer, I see it's a picnic basket.

"We're having a picnic?" I ask, looking around. "In the dark?"

"You'll see. C'mon."

We walk past the information center and head up a trail that leads to a rocky but steady area. Julian pulls a blanket out of the basket and drapes it over the ground so we can sit.

He pulls out two thermoses, which I quickly learn contain delicious coffee. Then, he wraps his arm around me, and I cuddle into his side. A few minutes later, just like magic, the sun begins to rise as we watch the darkness turn to light, exposing the most beautiful view that I will remember for the rest of my life.

Julian Parker might be my fake fiancé, but he's doing a damn good job at creating very real memories.

Twenty-One

JULIAN

"WOULD IT BE COMPLETELY UNPROFESSIONAL IF I called out sick tomorrow?" Ana groans as we step through the door.

It's been a long day of travel, and since it's only Monday, we're due back in the office tomorrow morning.

"Probably. But as your boss, I might be able to be persuaded to let you take the day off."

I smirk at her, and she glares my way.

"Ha-ha. Very funny." She rolls her luggage to the steps and is about to carry it up herself when I grab it from her and carry them both up.

She stops at her room, but I keep going with her luggage to my room.

"Um, hello? You passed my room," she calls after me. "Did you forget where my room was?"

She tries to grab her luggage, but I step in front of it so she can't get to it.

"What the hell are you doing, Julian?" she accuses. "I'm tired, and I need to unpack, shower, and get some sleep."

"And you can do that," I tell her, knowing damn well what I'm about to say next is going to have her flippin' her shit. "In here."

As my words sink in, her eyes widen, and her features morph from annoyed and exhausted to downright frightened.

"Julian," she whispers, "what the hell are you talking about?"

"You know exactly what I'm talking about. We just spent the past several nights in the same bed. There's no way in hell I'm going back to sleeping without you."

"All my stuff is in the other room."

"That can be fixed." I shrug. "But tomorrow because I'm exhausted too. I want to shower, fuck you in my bed, and then pass out with you next to me."

"I'm not sharing a bed with you."

"Why?"

"Because … because that's too … much!"

"Red," I deadpan, "I've been fucking you for days, in every hole, until we both passed out every night with you in my arms and your body wrapped around mine."

She stares at me like I've grown two heads, completely speechless, so I use that moment to pick her up and carry her to the bathroom.

This is the moment when most couples would have a conversation. They would discuss what they were to each other, admit they'd fallen for each other, and slap a label on the relationship.

But with Ana, things need to be done differently. Laying a claim to her will send her ass running. Giving us a label will scare the hell out of her. She'll question and second-guess everything.

So, instead, I'm not going to say shit. I'm going to show her every day how good we are together, and when the time comes for her dad to pick one of us to take over, we'll deal with it then. I want the CEO position, but for the first time, I also want something more. And if I have it my way, I'll get to have them both.

"Julian, what are you doing?" Ana gasps when I set her on the counter and turn the water on.

Because we're both tired, I carry her into the shower with me and rinse the day off both of us quickly.

We dry off, and since we didn't bring any clothes into the bathroom, we wrap our towels around us and head back out to the bedroom.

I see the determined glint in her eyes, ready to bolt out the door to her room, so I cut her off before she can make it out.

"Julian, I'm ..."

Her words trail off when I rip the towel off her body and then toss her onto my mattress.

Tugging my towel off as well, I climb up onto the bed and part her thighs.

With one hand on either side of her face, I rain kisses along her dewy, heated flesh. She smells like my body wash, and the caveman in me fucking loves it.

"Should I drag it out by playing with each part of your gorgeous body?" I ask, leaning down and taking a nipple between my teeth. I tug on it hard enough to make her cry out and then release it. "Or should I go straight to making you scream my name?"

I scoot down the bed and spread her thighs wider, giving me the perfect view of her cleanly shaven pussy.

"Which one?" I ask, raising a questioning brow.

"Just hurry up and make me come," she demands, thinking that she's punishing me by pushing things along since she's mad that I'm holding her hostage in my room.

But she'll soon learn that I don't give a shit because my favorite thing to do is make her scream my name. And once she's turned on, she turns into a fucking sex kitten.

"Your wish is my command, baby."

I delve between her legs and work her body over, licking and sucking and finger-fucking her pussy. She tries to refrain from making any noises, but when I stick a finger in her asshole, she loses the battle and moans in pleasure.

Her fingers pluck her nipples while I eat her pussy with vigor, not stopping until she's screaming my name and begging for more.

Only once her orgasm has subsided do I give her one last lick, wanting the taste to linger on my tongue, and then I lean back, giving her a moment to catch her breath.

"Ready for bed?" I ask, knowing damn well she wants more. An orgasm is nice, but my woman loves a good dicking.

She glares at me, wanting to be stubborn, but then she turns over and gets on all fours. "I want it in my ass," she says, glancing back.

I've learned this week that my woman loves anal sex, and she isn't shy about it.

"What happened to being tired?" I give her ass a playful smack and then slide my cock through her wet folds, coating my shaft with her juices.

"I am tired," she murmurs, giving me the sexiest pout, "but I want it in my ass."

"Only on one condition," I say, spreading her cheeks and gliding my cock up so it's resting against her tight pink rim. "You sleep in here with me."

I push the head into her ass slightly, just enough to spread the hole and give her a taste of what she can have if she plays nice.

"Okay!" she moans. "I'll sleep in here with you tonight. Just fuck my ass, please."

"Every night," I counter as I push the head in a bit more.

When she doesn't agree, I pull it away, and she glares back at me.

"Fine. I'll sleep with you in this bed every night. Now, fuck my ass!"

Reaching over, I grab the lube from my nightstand and squirt some onto her ass crack, then spread her cheeks and watch as the liquid descends straight to her puckered hole.

"Is this what you want, baby?" I taunt, pushing a single digit into her hole to get it nice and slick.

"Yes," she whispers. "Please."

I stroke my shaft a few times to make sure it'll slide in easily, and then grabbing and fisting her ponytail, I guide my cock into her tight hole, watching as she takes me so goddamn perfectly.

"Oh God, yes!" she cries once I'm all the way in. "Fuck me, please. Fuck me *hard*."

"You got it," I tell her as I start to fuck her ass just how she wants it.

What's that saying? *She's a lady in the streets, but a freak in the sheets*? That's exactly what Ana is, and I fucking love it. Love that she can saunter into a meeting in her red-soled heels like a badass bitch and own the room, and then behind closed doors, she demands for me to fuck her ass. This woman is as perfect as it gets, and she's going to soon figure out that I have no intention of letting her go.

Since we're going to need another shower after I've brought her to an orgasm, I pull out and flip her onto her back.

She takes one look at me and knows exactly what I want without me having to say a word.

Sitting up slightly, she grabs my shaft and strokes it until I'm painting her chest and neck with my cum.

And then, just when I think she can't get any more perfect, she opens her mouth and lets me finish on her tongue.

"So, what do you say, boss?" she says with a glint in her eyes. "Have I earned tomorrow off?"

Gripping her chin, I lean over and kiss her mouth, tasting the saltiness from my cum on her tongue. "Fuck no, baby. You've earned the entire week off."

Twenty-Two

ANASTASIA

"This Sunday, barbecue at our house."

I glance up from what I was working on and blink several times. *Our house.*

"Are you asking or telling?" I say, pushing his word choice to the side. I'll analyze that later.

"My family wants to meet you, and I haven't seen them since you moved in." He steps inside my office and closes the door behind him. "Figured it would be better to do it at our place than theirs."

There goes the whole "our" thing again ... but before I can focus too hard on that, the other part of his statement hits me.

"Your parents want to meet me?" I ask, trying to keep my tone level despite my sudden nervousness at the thought of meeting his mom and stepdad.

"Yeah. You can invite your dad and Selene. I might invite Ryder and his wife. We can make it a casual get-together. I'll grill." He winks playfully, but I'm still stuck on one thing …

"I've never met anyone's parents before."

"Well, there's a first for everything. My parents caught wind that I've met someone and that it's serious. So, they want to meet her. And since her is *you* …"

"Do they know …" I lift my left hand to show him my engagement ring.

"That we're engaged? Yeah. Nora is an attention whore and had the *Rosemary News* post a wedding announcement, which included pictures from the event. Since Ryder's family is a big deal around here, it was a main article, and it mentioned my fiancée and me attending." He shrugs like this is no big deal. "My sister called this morning, hurt that I didn't tell her, and then she and my mom tag-teamed me this afternoon by video calling me on three-way and begging to meet you."

"Great," I mutter. "So, they already hate me."

"What?" Julian walks farther into my office. "Why would you say that?"

"Because we got engaged behind their back. My mom would be so upset if she were still alive and I did that."

"They'll get over it once you hit them with all that charm." He slides between me and my desk and pinches my chin, lifting my face up. "You won me over in a matter of minutes, Red, and I have no doubt you'll do the same to my family."

He leans down and presses a soft kiss to my lips, and I sigh into it, not caring that we're at work. We've been back from Hawaii for a few weeks now, and if I thought things would go back to *normal* once we were home—you know, pre-Hawaii days—I was wrong.

We might not be living in the vacation bubble anymore, but that hasn't stopped Julian from pretending like we're still there. Sure, we go to work every day, but at five o'clock on the dot, he insists we leave—oh, did I mention he somehow conned me into carpooling with him? Yep, we're *that* couple.

We spend the evening either ordering in, him cooking, or on occasion, we go out. We talk and laugh, and he never lets us discuss work.

Sometimes, we watch a movie. Other nights, I lie on the couch with my head in his lap while we both read our separate books. The night always ends with him fucking me until I'm so tired that I can barely speak, and then after we shower, I fall asleep in his arms.

I'm almost positive that he's attempting to fuck me into submission, but it's so good that I don't have it in me to argue. Besides, we only have a few months until my dad makes his decision at the end of the year, so I might as well enjoy it while I can because even though Julian won't admit it, I know damn well once my dad picks one of us, whatever this is between us will come to a screeching halt.

"So, what do you say?" he asks, shaking me out of my thoughts. "Barbecue at our place?" He strokes down my cheek with his knuckles. "It would mean a lot to me. I'm close with my family, and I want you guys to get to know each other. They're important to me ... and so are you."

"Sure," I choke out, refusing to think about how deep his statement runs. Standing between his legs, I wrap my arms around his neck, needing to lighten the mood. "On one condition," I say, using his words from a few weeks ago against him. "You fuck me on my desk and make me come at least twice."

"Oh, Red." He chuckles. "Just for that, I'm not going to stop until you've come three times."

"Do I look okay?"

I glance down at the fourth sundress I've changed into and then back up at Julian, who has the nerve to chuckle.

"You look beautiful. Hell, you could wear a potato sack, and you'd still be the most gorgeous woman in the room."

I roll my eyes and pull the dress off, throwing it onto the bed. "That's cliché and annoying, Julian Parker. I'm meeting your entire family today. You don't get it because you might as well be the son my dad always wanted, but this is scary." I shouldn't be this nervous to meet my fake future in-laws, yet I am.

"My family's going to love you," he says just as the doorbell rings, and I shriek in surprise.

"They're early!" I gasp, grabbing the dress I just took off and sliding it back on.

"Probably. Frank has this weird saying: *To be early is to be on time, to be on time is to be late, and to be late is to be forgotten.*"

"Jesus," I hiss, quickly sliding on my sandals. "My mom used to say it's better to arrive late than to arrive ugly," I mutter, reapplying my red lipstick.

Julian laughs, and I glare.

"Breathe," he says, kissing my cheek. "Everything's going to go great."

We rush down the stairs, and just before he opens the door, I grab his arm and glance at him.

"Don't forget, if anyone asks, I made all the side dishes and desserts."

He rolls his eyes but nods. "My fiancée is not only a badass marketing analyst, but she's also a cuisinier." He grins. "Got it."

After trying to cook several dishes to impress his mom and sister—who love to cook and bake and, according to him, are damn good at it—and burning and ruining every one, I gave up and ordered from a local restaurant and bakery.

Julian swings open the door and says, "Mom, Frank!" He gives them each a hug while I stand back, my heart beating rapidly in my chest. "I'd love for you to meet my fiancée, Anastasia. This is my mom, Helen, and my stepdad, Frank."

"You can call me Ana," I tell them, extending my hand.

Helen glances down at it in confusion, then steps inside and wraps her arms around me in a hug. "It's so great to finally meet you," she says, then steps back. "My goodness, you're even prettier in person."

"Oh, well, thank you. It's lovely to meet you both." I glance from Helen to Frank. "Julian has told me so much about you."

"All good, I hope," a young woman says, sauntering through the door. Unlike Julian's brown hair, hers is blonde, but she has the same emerald eyes he and their mom have. "What's up, big bro?" She kisses him on the cheek, and he rolls his eyes. "It's been too long. I started to get worried when you weren't bugging me about my classes every five seconds, like you usually do."

"Ana, this bane of my existence is my baby sister, Jessika."

"His favorite sister," she argues.

"My only sister."

"That you know of," she retorts, making her brother grumble.

"It's nice to meet you." Jessika gives me a quick hug and smiles. "I didn't think we'd ever see the day that Mr. Workaholic would actually settle down, but now, I get it. You're gorgeous."

"And smart," Julian says, pulling me into his side. "Ana has her degree in business marketing and her MBA in hospitality."

Jessika's eyes go wide. "Oh, so you're not a trophy wife, huh? I didn't see that one coming."

"Jessika!" Helen hisses. "I'm sorry," she apologizes. "My daughter has no filter."

"It's okay," I say, freaking out at how badly this is going. "I'm definitely not trophy-wife material. Hell, I'm not even sure I'm wife material," I joke and then cringe at how horrible that sounded.

"What I meant is …" I swallow nervously, trying to come up with a way to save this train wreck, but I draw a blank.

"What she meant is," Julian says, "she'd rather be running a company than doing laundry. And it's one of the things I love about her." He glances down at me with mirth twinkling in his eyes. "She's my biggest competition for the CEO position."

"Oh," his mom says. "I didn't know you worked together. Julian said you met online …"

"We did," I admit. "But it turns out that my dad is his boss."

"Samuel Kingston is your father?" Frank says, glancing from me to Julian in confusion. "Why haven't we seen you at any of the company functions?"

"I was away," I mutter, wondering how the hell we got here in less than two minutes while still standing in the foyer.

Spotting the dishes in Frank's hands, I say, "Can I take those from you?" hoping to change the subject and get this barbecue back on track.

Frank hands them over. "Thank you. I don't know what's in there, but if I were to get mugged, I could probably hit him and knock him out."

Jessika snorts. "In this neighborhood? They'd probably think we were the ones trying to mug them."

She glances my way with a glimmer in her eye, and I quickly excuse myself to put the dishes in the kitchen before she can make a comment about me being born rich and privileged since she now knows I'm a Kingston.

I set the dishes on the counter, unsure of what the hell to do with them, but thankfully, Julian follows me and lifts the lids to check them out.

"Mmm, mac 'n' cheese. That will go perfectly with the burgers I'm grilling."

"I know it's your favorite," his mom says sweetly from behind us. "The other dish is a homemade apple pie."

"Hell yeah," Julian says. "Good thing Ana bough—*made* other desserts because this pie is all mine."

"Oh! What did you make?" Helen asks.

"Lemon bars and, um, cake pops."

I made sure everything *looked* like it could be homemade.

"Sounds yummy," Helen says as the doorbell rings again.

"I'll get it," I offer, leaving Julian with his family.

I open the door, expecting my dad and Selene, but instead find Ryder and his wife, Nora, standing there, both looking like they'd rather be anywhere but here.

"Hello," I say, putting on my best hostess smile. "I'm so glad you could make it."

"Thank you for having us," Nora says, sticking a fake smile on her face.

Just as they walk through the door, my dad and Selene come around the corner.

"Anastasia," my dad says, opening his arms to hug me. "Thank you for the invite."

"Thanks for coming."

I finish giving him a hug and then give Selene one. I don't know her well, but every time I'm around her, she's always so nice. I can see why my dad loves her.

After introductions are made, Julian herds everyone outside and offers them a drink. Jessika lies out by the pool with her mom while Frank offers to help Julian man the grill, and my dad and Selene sit at the table with Nora and Ryder.

As I stand here, wondering what the hell I'm supposed to be doing, it hits me how long it's been since I've had to be social. When my parents were married, Mom would host parties all the time. Until they started drifting apart and she stopped. Then, it was as if an invisible line had been drawn, and while Dad would still have his functions and dinners, Mom and I never attended—which is why I never met Julian or his family. Soon after, I left for college and then London, not returning until now.

Living in London meant focusing on school and work. The only reason I became friends with Paige was because we worked together. For the past several years, I've been an introvert, and I didn't realize until now how much it's affected me. I used to be the life of the party, but now, I feel like I barely belong.

As if Julian can sense my hesitancy, his gaze roams across the expansive backyard and finds me. He smiles softly and nods once, beckoning me over to him. And like a moth to a flame, I go.

"I was just telling my dad how you spent the past several years in London," Julian says, sliding the arm he's not using to grill across my shoulders and pulling me into his side. "He wants to take my mom there for their anniversary. Any pointers?"

I spend the next several minutes sharing my favorite parts of England while Julian grills. I can't help but notice that the entire time, he makes it a point to touch me. Whether it's to kiss my temple or squeeze my hip, he constantly keeps the connection going. I've never considered myself an affectionate person, but with every touch and kiss, I find myself craving more. And it's in that moment that I realize I'm falling for Julian. It wasn't planned—if anything, it only complicates things—but it doesn't change the fact that it's happening.

"Food will be ready in about ten minutes," Julian says, snapping me from my thoughts. "Wanna go heat up the sides and set them out?"

"Sure," I rasp, my emotions clogging my throat.

I step away from him, but before I can get far, he pulls me back into his arms and presses a quick kiss to my lips.

"What was that for?" I ask.

"Just needed my Ana fix to hold me over."

He playfully winks, and I feel my face heating up, suddenly shy with his dad watching and chuckling next to us.

When I get to the kitchen, I go about grabbing the dishes I bought to look like I made them and heat them up as the manager at the restaurant explained to do. I also throw in the mac 'n' cheese Helen made.

While they heat up, I work on getting the outside area set up to eat. Once everything's hot, I create a buffet of sorts. Julian comes over with the burgers and chicken, and everyone starts to fill their plates.

"Ana, this sweet potato casserole is delicious!" my dad exclaims from across the table. "Where did you get it from?"

"She made it," Julian says as he stuffs his face with a forkful of mac 'n' cheese. "She made all of it."

He shoots me a quick wink, and my heart swells at him having my back. I might not be wife material, but Julian is definitely husband material.

"Oh, wow," Helen says. "I'll have to get the recipes from you."

"Really?" Nora adds, furrowing her brows in mock contemplation while I hold my breath, praying she's not about to say what I think she's about to say ... and then she says it. "It tastes an awful lot like the sweet potato casserole from Maggie's. As a matter of fact, so does the pasta salad and the fruit salad." She smirks. "Are you sure you actually made these? Because I'm pretty sure when I ate there a few weeks ago—"

"Enough," Julian barks as tears of embarrassment prick my eyes.

"Excuse me," I rush out, standing to get away before I cry in front of everyone. "I think I forgot ... something."

I run from the table, not stopping until I get to the guest bathroom and lock myself in. I don't know what I was thinking, lying about cooking. I should've just said I bought it, and nobody would've cared.

As I swipe at the tears that are sliding down my cheeks, there's a soft knock on the door. Assuming it's Julian, I wipe under my eyes and then crack the door open.

Only it's not Julian.

"Helen," I gasp.

"Can we talk?"

She smiles softly, and I step out and follow her to the living room, where she sits on the couch and pats the cushion next to her for me to join.

"The lunch was delicious."

"Thanks." I snort out a self-deprecating laugh. "But as you heard, I didn't make it. The truth is, I can't cook or clean or do laundry."

"Why did you lie?" she asks, zero judgment in her tone.

"Because I wanted to impress you," I admit truthfully. "Julian thinks the world of you. The way you take care of your family. You taught them how to cook and clean and do laundry." I shrug sheepishly.

"I wanted you to think I was capable of taking care of him as well. You're, like, the perfect wife and mom," I mutter. "Meanwhile, I can barely boil a pot of water without burning it."

"Oh, Ana," she says, taking my hand in hers and squeezing it. "First of all, nobody is perfect. And there are many other ways to take care of someone."

"How?"

"Well, sometimes, taking care of someone is as simple as loving them. I've only been around you and my son for a short time, but I can see a huge change in him. He laughs and smiles more. He can't keep his eyes off of you."

As she speaks, her admission swirls around in my head, making me dizzy. She thinks Julian loves me? I know he's mentioned wanting to see where things could go between us, but love? Is it possible?

"So what if you don't do all the domestic stuff?" she continues. "You make him happy, and as his mom, that's all that matters to me ... that my children are happy."

"And that's all that matters to me," Julian says, making me jump in my seat.

"Mom, can you give me a moment with Ana, please?" he adds, walking over to stand next to me.

"Of course." She smiles at him. Then, she turns back to me and says, "If you ever want to learn how to cook or bake, I'd love to teach you, but if that's not something that interests you, that's okay too."

"Thank you," I tell her. "That means a lot to me."

Once Julian and I are alone, I lean back and groan. "Not exactly how I hoped today would go."

"Eh"—he chuckles—"could've gone worse."

"Really?" I hiss, glancing over at him. "How so?"

"You could've served the food you made and given everyone food poisoning."

He shrugs, and I glare his way, not finding his joke funny in the slightest.

"I hate you."

I smack his chest, and he grabs my hand, pulling me into his lap so I'm straddling his thighs.

"No, you don't," he says, leaning in and kissing me. "You like me," he singsongs. "You really, really like me."

"How do you figure?" I mutter.

"It's simple," he says with a grin. "You lied about cooking the food to impress my family. You wanted your soon-to-be in-laws to like you … because you like me."

"There's nothing simple about anything you just said."

"That's where you're wrong, Red." Julian cradles my face in his palms. "You're trying to complicate shit, but the truth is, everything about us is really fucking simple, and the sooner you realize it, the quicker we'll be able to move forward." He kisses the tip of my nose.

"But don't worry, Red. I'm in no rush. Take all the time you need to figure out what I already know."

"And what's that?" I breathe.

"That you and I are inevitable."

Twenty-Three

JULIAN

"WITH THE TIMELINE WE'RE WORKING WITH, I'D probably say ..."

Ana strolls into my office, stopping me mid-thought as I rake my gaze down her body. I had to be at work early for a meeting this morning, so I didn't see her before I left. She's dressed in a sexy black pencil skirt, a white button-down blouse, and a pair of fuck-me heels. I briefly wonder if I can convince her to let me slide that skirt up and over her ass and fuck her from behind with her bent over my—

"Jesus, man," Ryder says, reminding me that he's in my office. "I can practically hear your dirty thoughts from here." He stands and shakes his head. "We can finish this conversation later ... when you're not busy fantasizing about your fiancée."

"You don't have to leave on my account," Ana says.

"I need to get home anyway," he tells her. "Nora is craving chocolate-covered pickles and swears if I don't somehow find a way to get them for her, she'll die." His eyes widen at his slipup. "I mean …"

"I already told her."

"And I won't tell anyone," she promises.

"Thanks. We're announcing it soon. I'm sure you'll be invited to the party." He rolls his eyes. "Speaking of parties, have fun in Vegas … but not too much fun."

"Yes, *Daddy*," I say, making Ana laugh and Ryder glare.

He leaves, closing the door behind him, and I turn my attention to Ana.

"To what do I owe the pleasure of you visiting my office?" I smirk playfully. "Hoping to get fucked? Because I can make that happen."

She snorts out a laugh and drops a file onto my desk. "The day-care plans have been drawn up by the architect and approved by the engineer for the remodel. I need you to sign off on them."

"Okay, cool," I say, pulling her into my lap. "I'll look over these on the plane tomorrow. Now, what do you say to me bending you over this desk and fucking that perfect pussy of yours until you come?"

"Mmm." She grinds against me. "I would say—"

Buzz.

"Mr. Parker, sorry for the interruption, but you told me to let you know if Sonia calls. She's on line one."

"Shit, I need to take this."

I pat Ana's butt, and she pouts, but this call is too important to blow off.

"Seriously, you go from wanting to have office sex to dismissing me?" she says as she stands with a huff.

"Sorry, I need to take this call. Rain check?"

"Whatever," she grumbles. "I'm heading home to finish packing. Maybe I'll pull out my pink vibrator and give it a go. B.O.B. has been feeling a bit left out."

"Touch yourself, and you'll regret it," I warn, the thought of her coming without me making me see red.

"Oh, really? Then, you'd better get home quickly to stop me," she sasses, sauntering out and slamming the door behind her with a cackle.

I grab the receiver, hoping this call is quick so I can chase after my woman. I planned to stay late to get some shit done since we're leaving first thing tomorrow morning for Vegas, but my priorities have shifted— number one: getting home to make my gorgeous fiancée come.

"Sonia," I say when I answer. "What can I do for you?"

"You can meet me for dinner at Carlson's tonight."

Well, shit, there goes my night.

ANASTASIA

"You can meet me for dinner at Carlson's tonight."

I stop in my place as a sultry voice practically purrs the words over the speakerphone to my fiancé.

"Whoops." Josie quickly lifts and drops the receiver, silencing the call. "I forgot to click transfer," she says with a nervous smile that has my hackles rising. "With the new system, if I don't click ..."

She rambles on, but my only focus is on the fact that some woman seems to think Julian is going to meet her at Carlson's when he's meeting me at the house.

My phone dings with a text, and I pull it out, finding a message from Julian that has my heart plummeting into my stomach.

JULIAN

A last-minute meeting came up.
I'll probably be home late.

ME

Guess the vibrator it is.

JULIAN

I'll make it up to you. I promise.

JULIAN

You should have dinner with your dad since
we're leaving tomorrow for a few days.

"Who's Sonia?" I ask Josie, pocketing my phone.

"I'm not sure," she says with a shrug. "Julian just told me to put her through to him, no matter what."

"You're his assistant. Shouldn't you know who he does business with?" I accuse, my tone harsh.

"I don't know everything about Julian," she snaps back. "Take you, for example. I didn't know about you until you two were already engaged. Now, if you'll excuse me, I have work to do."

I should probably apologize, but I'm too upset about the fact that my fiancée is going out with another woman tonight instead of coming home and being with me.

On the way home, I call Paige, needing to speak to someone who's not associated with Julian.

"Hello, stranger," she says. "How's it going?"

"I think Julian is cheating on me."

"Can he do that if your engagement is fake?"

I open my mouth, then close it, unsure of how to answer that because she's right. Our engagement is fake, so technically, he's not cheating on me. But …

"He told me he wanted us to be real," I whisper, my heart cracking into pieces.

"Oh," she gasps. "Apparently, a lot has happened since we last spoke. Care to get me caught up?"

I quickly give her the CliffsNotes version, and when I'm done, she whistles under her breath.

"Never thought I'd see the day."

"What?"

"The all-work, no-play Anastasia Webb has fallen in love."

"I have not." But even as I deny it, I know I'm lying to myself because she's right. I have fallen for Julian. Despite everything, I have fallen for my fake fiancé, who apparently thinks it's okay to date other women.

"Maybe since you're not official, he doesn't think he's doing anything wrong," Paige suggests.

"He told me the first day we met that he would be loyal," I hiss. "And now, he's talking to other women, but expects me to give us a real chance? Fuck that."

"Then, maybe it's a business meeting," Paige says. "You should just talk to him."

I'm about to pull into the driveway, but at the last second, I pass it by.

"I'm going to Carlson's."

"And what are you going to do if you find him with another woman?"

"I don't know," I whisper, the thought making me sick to my stomach. "But I need to know."

The drive to Carlson's feels like it takes forever. Once I arrive, I let the valet attendant know I won't be long so he doesn't park my vehicle. Then, I go in search of Julian.

I find him quickly, sitting in a corner booth with a beautiful blonde woman. I stand, frozen in place, while I watch them talk and laugh. He drinks his scotch, no doubt Kingston Gold Label, while she sips her glass of white wine.

When she leans over and places her hand on his arm while looking at him like he hung the damn moon, I can't take it anymore and leave. A myriad of emotions flits through me on the way home—heartbroken, sad, hurt, devastated, and confused—but the one I settle on is betrayed.

How dare he make me fall for him, only to seek out another woman! I might not be perfect, but I deserve better than that.

I finish packing despite not wanting to go on this trip. I'm going to be stuck on a plane with Julian for three hours and then sharing a room with him for the next three nights.

Twenty-Four

ANASTASIA

Julian's strong arms wrap around me from behind, and for a second, I forget about what I saw and allow myself to sink back into him, getting lost in the comfort of his touch and warmth.

He nuzzles his face into the crook of my neck, and I tilt my head slightly to give him better access. As he trails kisses along my flesh, I let out a needy moan, wanting more.

I never knew how cold and lonely sleeping alone was until I spent the past month sleeping in the same bed as Julian. The thought of going back to sleeping alone is sad and depressing. But instead of allowing those emotions to settle within me, I push them out and focus on the emotion that's easier to hide behind—anger.

And then he speaks, and his words are enough to set me off.

"I know it's late, and I should probably let you sleep," he murmurs. "But I need to know, baby, did you get off without me?"

Pushing off him, I roll to the other side of the bed and slide off, needing to get away from him. It's too hard to be strong with his body wrapped around mine and his scent invading my senses.

"I need to use the bathroom," I mutter, unable to look at him.

I snatch my phone off the nightstand and lock myself in the bathroom. When I see it's after two in the morning, it takes everything in me not to stomp back out and demand Julian admit to what he's done. But after googling how to handle a cheater, I learned that most cheaters would lie anyway, so it's pointless. What's done is done—lesson learned.

Since we have to get up in a couple of hours to head to the airport anyway, after I go pee and wash my hands, I jump in the shower to prolong facing Julian. I hear the doorknob jiggle, but thankfully, I had the foresight to lock it.

I take my time blow-drying and straightening my hair, and then I put on my makeup, going a bit darker and edgier and making sure my red lipstick is perfect. Once I'm ready for battle, I step into the bedroom with my robe wrapped around me.

Only, when my eyes land on Julian, I find him passed out in bed. Of course he is. Probably wore himself out fucking Sonia.

I quickly get dressed and then spend the rest of the morning in my makeshift office. I couldn't even tell you what I'm working on, but the only way I know to distract myself is to delve into work. Hours pass by, and the next thing I know, Julian is leaning against the doorframe, watching me.

"Is it time to go?" I ask, still refusing to make eye contact with him.

"Yeah."

Taking a deep breath, I pack my laptop and charger and then walk to the door with my head held high, hoping he'll let me by without stopping me.

And for a moment, I think he's actually going to— until, at the last second, he extends his arm, blocking the doorway.

"Excuse me," I say, trying like hell not to let my emotions seep through. "I need to get by."

"Not until you tell me what the hell is going on."

"We need to go so we don't miss our flight."

"It's a private plane," he drawls, "with your last name across the side. It's not going anywhere without us. So, let me ask you again, and this time, don't deflect. What the hell is going on?"

"I don't want to talk about it right now," I tell him, doing my best to remain strong while, inside, I'm trembling.

I've learned from this ordeal that refraining from being in relationships might mean being lonely and not getting laid as often, but it also means not risking having your heart ripped out of your chest.

"Ana," Julian says softly, "if you don't tell me what's wrong, I can't fix it."

"It can't be fixed," I choke out, suddenly feeling sick to my stomach. "Now, please move."

He sighs, but drops his arm, respecting my wishes, and I take off down the hall to grab my luggage and go to the car that's waiting to bring us to the airport.

The car ride and plane ride are intense, the tension so thick that you could cut it with a knife, but Julian doesn't say a word to me the entire time. Instead, he just stares at me, like he'll somehow be able to reach into my head and get answers.

When we arrive in Vegas, another car is waiting to take us to the hotel we're staying at. The rest of the day flies by, both of us working our asses off with our team to make sure everything is perfect for Saturday night. And when Julian and I stumble into our room, he doesn't even try to get answers from me.

We both shower, and then early the next morning, we do it all over again. Only tonight, we're meeting Ronan and his team for dinner. Thankfully, we've agreed that when it comes to work events, we behave professionally, which means Julian needs to keep his distance despite Ronan knowing we're engaged.

We have dinner in a private suite, where we reveal Ronan's personalized whiskey.

"Damn, you guys are good," Ronan says as he and his team try Kingston's Ronan Flynn Limited Edition Irish Whiskey. "This is smooth with the perfect amount of malt."

"That's our job," I tell him. "Now, for your drink."

I nod toward the waiters, and they bring out glasses of *Mo Ghrá*—meaning *my love* in Irish—which takes him back to his roots. His mom is from Ireland, and she was the reason he fell so deeply in love with music. She passed away last year, and he wanted to honor her and his love of music.

"This is your signature Irish whiskey, mixed with one of our top dry red wines and a touch of orange."

Ronan takes a sip and grins, nodding in satisfaction. "You guys nailed it."

"That's what we like to hear," Julian says. "This drink will be served at the club opening tomorrow night, along with bottles of Ronan Flynn Limited Edition."

We spend the next couple of hours eating and drinking while discussing the specifics. I let Julian take over while I drink my weight in alcohol, hoping it will help dull the constant pain in my chest.

When dinner is over and we part ways, instead of going up to our room, I head down to the casino bar to drink some more. I'm two, maybe three drinks in when Julian sits in the seat next to me.

"This seat is taken," I mutter.

"Yeah, by me."

Since it'll be easier for me to leave than argue with him to go, I finish off the last of my drink and stand. I already gave the bartender our room number so he can charge my drinks there. I drop a twenty onto the bar top as a tip and walk away, unsure of where to go.

Before I can make it too far though, Julian grabs me by my hip and pulls me into a darkened hall, pushing me up against the wall.

"I've given you your space, but I've had enough," he says, caging me in his arms, his palms resting on either side of my head and his knee nestled between my thighs. "What the fuck did I do that has you acting like this?"

"I don't even know why you care," I hiss. "Wouldn't your time be better spent with *Sonia*?"

Julian's brows furrow in confusion. "What the fuck are you talking about?"

"I'm talking about the gorgeous blonde I saw all over you at Carlson's. Tell me this … does she know you're engaged?"

The corner of Julian's mouth quirks like he's about to smirk, but he tamps it down quickly. "You saw us at Carlson's?" he asks, ignoring my question. "Why didn't you come over and say something?"

"I figured three was a crowd." I glare, and this time, he doesn't hide it when he barks out a laugh.

"Oh, fuck, Red. You're jealous."

"I'm not jealous," I spit. "I just don't like to play games. If you want to fuck her, go for it. But don't crawl into bed afterward, expecting me to spread my legs for you."

I try to wiggle out of Julian's hold, but he lifts his knee, pushing the bottom of my dress up and grinding it against the apex of my legs as his hip pins me against the wall, stopping me from going anywhere.

"Let's get one thing straight," he murmurs, his eyes locking on mine. "The *only* woman I'm fucking is you." One of his hands lowers to between my legs, and he rubs me in the perfect way that has me releasing a traitorous moan. "And I'd better be the only man you're fucking."

"Then, who the hell is she?" I argue. "Because I'm not stupid and I saw her touching you."

"She is Sonia Rodriguez, the chief marketing and strategy officer for the Houston Flyers."

"The NBA team?"

"Yep. I met her through a business acquaintance, and with the NBA season starting soon, I told her I could meet whenever she was available. She'd been out of town, and she said she could meet Wednesday night, and considering we were heading to Vegas, I didn't want to reschedule.

"She was touching you," I mutter, sounding like a child, but I know what I saw.

"She did," he admits, continuing to rub friction between my legs.

With the material of my panties being so thin, it's like there's nothing between my pussy and his material-clad knee. And if he keeps this up, I'm going to come all over his knee, right here in the hotel casino.

His admission snaps me out of my fog, and I push his knee away.

"Why the fuck would you let her touch you?"

He grins, and if I were a violent woman, I would smack that smile right off his face.

"I love every side of you, Red. The passionate workaholic, the feisty fighter, the soft lover, but I must say, the jealous side of you has me so damn hard."

He takes my hand in his and pushes it against his crotch to show me, and despite my being pissed at him, my mouth waters, wanting to wrap my lips around his hard length and remind him who he belongs to.

Oh shit. *Who he belongs to* ... because ...

"You're mine," I breathe, speaking the first honest words regarding us since we started this whole mess of a thing.

"Damn straight I am," he says, palming my cheek affectionately. "And that's exactly what I told her. And if you hadn't run, jumping to conclusions, then you would've known that."

"I ..." I shake my head, feeling like a fool. "I'm usually smarter than this. I'm a numbers person. I deal with data and statistics. I base my decisions on facts and research. But this whole relationship thing is driving me nuts."

"Because falling in love isn't a math equation you can solve," he says with a hint of humor in his tone. "It comes from in here." He presses his hand on the area above my heart. "Feelings can't be analyzed. You have to go with how you feel."

"Love?" I whisper. "Do you love me?"

"Yeah, Ana," he says. "I love you. I've fallen in love with you, every part of you. The good, the bad, the stubborn, the workaholic, and the soft part of you that you only let a small number of people see, including me."

Oh my God. Julian Parker is in love with me. He sees me and gets me and accepts me, and in spite of it all, he still loves me.

"Why aren't you mad at me?" I ask curiously. "You have every right to be. I just accused you of cheating without any proof." If I were in his position, I'd be pissed at the false accusation.

"Because when I told you I'd wait, I meant it. From the first time we spoke, I knew you wouldn't be an easy catch, but I've learned over the years that most things in life don't come easy, and you're worth it."

He leans in and brushes a kiss to my lips, and I wrap my arms around his neck.

He deepens our connection, slipping his tongue into my mouth so I can taste the whiskey on his breath, and then he lifts me up, pressing me harder into the wall while I wrap my legs around his waist.

"If it were up to me, Red," he murmurs against my mouth, "I'd marry you right now. That's how sure I am of us. How sure I am of the love I feel for you."

His admission shocks me, but not in the way I'd expect. Maybe it's the fact that I've been drinking—though I'm nowhere near drunk—but it's as if these feelings for him are burning bright and colorful in the dark, cold night, and I don't want them to disappear. I want to stoke the flames and fuel the fire. Now that I've felt the warmth, I don't want to go back to the cold. Now that I can see, I don't want to be blind.

"Okay," I blurt out.

"Okay what?" he says slowly, though based on the hopeful look in his eyes, he knows what I'm talking about.

"Let's get married."

"Are you serious right now? Don't fuck with me, Red," he warns.

"I'm serious," I tell him. "We're already engaged, and we're in Vegas. And ... I've fallen in love with you too. Let's do it, Julian. Let's get married."

Twenty-Five

JULIAN

"*I'VE FALLEN IN LOVE WITH YOU TOO.*"

Those words are the reason I've just married Anastasia Kingston. The reason we arrived at the Clark County Marriage License Bureau just before midnight and got our marriage license. The reason we found a small chapel and paid an officiant to read us our vows.

We laughed.

Ana shockingly shed a few tears.

We were pronounced husband and wife.

We kissed.

And now, we're back in our room with Ana laid out in the middle of the bed, naked and ready for me.

"Are you just going to stand there and stare at your *wife*, or are you going to fuck her and consummate this marriage?" She punctuates her question by reaching up and palming her bare breasts while smirking at me.

"I'm going to fuck my wife every damn day for the rest of our lives, but right now, I'm taking a moment to appreciate the view, Mrs. Parker."

Her eyes widen at the use of my last name, and she squirms in her spot.

"You like that?" I murmur, crawling onto the bed. I've already shed my clothes, and all that's left on me are my briefs. "Being called my name? It's like I own you." I spread her legs and expose her neatly trimmed cunt. "Like you're *mine*."

"Who said I'm changing my last name?" she sasses. "Maybe *you* should change your name to Kingston."

Some men prefer a submissive wife, one who obeys and goes with the flow. But not me. I love my feisty woman, who keeps me on my toes.

"Is that what you want?" I ask, swiping up her center with my fingertips. "You want me to change my last name to Kingston?"

"It is the better name," she chokes out.

"How about we play a game?" I suggest, coating my fingers with her juices. "The person who makes the other person come first gets to keep their last name, and the other person has to change theirs."

I lightly circle her clit, and her entire body shivers in response.

"Fine," she says. "But you don't get a head start."

She sits up and tugs on my briefs, so I shove them down my thighs. My hard cock springs out, ready to be inside my wife's warm, wet pussy.

She strokes my shaft a few times, and I let her, but there's no way I'm coming in her hand. So, before she can take it any further, I palm her ass cheeks and drop her back down onto her back.

Without giving her a second to react, I spread her thighs and slide down her body, my tongue landing directly on her clit. I lick and suck it, knowing exactly how to make my woman come.

Holding down her hips, I thrust two fingers into her warmth and devour her like a starved man. She thrashes about, screaming my name, torn between pleasure and anger, but it doesn't matter because within seconds, she's coming all over my fingers and tongue.

"I can't believe you!" she hisses, sitting up, her hazel eyes glassy from her orgasm.

"You can't believe what?" I argue. "That I would bring my A game when the stakes were that fucking high?" I crawl back over her, pushing gently on her chest so she's on her back once again. "What's your name, baby?"

She purses her lips together, refusing to give me what I want. It doesn't surprise me since my woman is a sore loser. I part her legs with one hand while I use the other to hold myself up, and then I guide my hard length into her hole. Her eyes roll back, and she moans softly.

Once I'm all the way in, I pull back out, and her eyes pop back open.

"What are you doing?" she breathes. "Fuck me."

"What's your name?"

"Serious—"

I thrust back into her, and she moans louder.

When I pull back out, she glares.

"C'mon, Red. All you gotta do is tell me your name, and I'll gladly make you come again."

Instead of entering her, I grip my shaft and stroke it up and down her sensitive clit, watching as she tries to win this battle. With her soaking wet, it creates the perfect amount of friction, and just before she's about to come for the second time, I break our contact, leaving her hanging.

"No!" she whines. "Please. I was so close."

"Just say the words, baby."

I lean over and press my lips to the corner of her mouth, and she grumbles under her breath. And then I kiss my way down her chest and pull one of her taut nipples into my mouth. I suck on it for several seconds, working her up. When her legs squeeze around me, I release her nipple.

"Okay! Okay!" she cries. "My name is Anastasia Parker. Now, please fuck—"

Before she can finish her sentence, I'm thrusting into her and giving her exactly what she wants.

Her legs wrap around me, and her arms snake around my neck, so we're connected in the most intimate way. She pulls my face to hers and kisses me with the same passion that I make love to her with as my wife for the first time.

She finds her release first and takes me with her, and as I come inside her perfect cunt, I whisper, "I love you," not expecting her to say anything back, but needing her to know how I feel.

But as we both take a moment to catch our breaths, my cock still inside her and her arms still wrapped around my neck, I'm shocked when she looks me in the eyes and says the words back. "I love you, Julian, and I'd be honored to be Mrs. Parker."

And just like that, I fall for my wife even harder.

ANASTASIA

I'm Mrs. Anastasia Parker.

One minute, I was wrongly accusing Julian of cheating, and the next, we were saying, "I do," in a quaint chapel just off the Strip, where we promised to love and honor each other for better or worse, until death do us part.

And then for the rest of the night, Julian and I made love to each other. I couldn't even tell you how many times I orgasmed or when we fell asleep, but judging by the way we're both naked, with Julian's body wrapped around mine and the area between my legs still sticky, I'd guess we passed out from exhaustion.

Not wanting to wake him up, I carefully remove his arms and slide out of the bed so I can shower and get cleaned up. Hopefully, I don't end up with an infection from falling asleep with his cum inside me. A glance at the clock tells me it's only been a few hours, so I should be okay.

As I stand under the water, with my eyes closed, breathing in the hot air, my memory floods back to the event from yesterday. I was so hurt at the thought of Julian allowing another woman to touch him and at the possibility that he did more with her.

I'm new to this whole committed-relationship thing, but he didn't get upset or annoyed. He didn't judge me for not being good at any of this. He handled it so well, with patience and understanding. And it was what made me finally admit to myself that I'd fallen in love with him.

The way we'd started was a bit complicated, but being with him—loving him and being loved by him—is easy. He was right. I was trying to complicate shit because I was scared. But I'm ready to be with him for real.

My thoughts skip forward to returning home, and I try to imagine what it will be like, being married to Julian. He'll definitely want me to move all of my stuff into his room. He already hates that I've left my clothes in his guest room despite sleeping in the same bed with him every night.

And we'll both need wedding bands. The officiant offered to sell us rings, but Julian declined, telling me that he wants my wedding band to match the engagement ring. I'll need to order him a wedding band once we're home. The thought of him wearing a black zirconium or maybe a platinum ring on his fourth finger to indicate he's taken is more of a turn-on than I thought it would be. But there's just something about knowing he's committed to me and only me. When everyone looks at his ring, they'll know—oh shit! Everyone ... including my dad!

When he finds out I ran to Vegas and got married, he's going to flip his shit.

"What's going through that beautiful head of yours, wife?" Julian asks, making me jump.

He steps into the shower and wraps his arms around me from behind, kissing my shoulder. "It looked like you were a thousand miles away."

"I was just thinking about last night," I tell him as my brain whirls with thoughts of having to tell my dad that I'm married.

He turns me around and glances down at me. "So, no regrets?"

When I hesitate, his brows furrow together. "Talk to me."

"We skipped so many steps," I say, "like dating, and went directly to living together. I don't regret it because it's our story, and not every story is the same ..."

"But ..." he prompts, worry etched on his features.

I try to figure out how to explain the thoughts that are going through my head, but no matter how I put it, it's going to sound bad.

"Ana, talk to me."

"First, we were fake engaged ... and then we got fake married."

Okay, that's not how it was supposed to come out.

But before I can do damage control, Julian takes a step back. "What the fuck are you talking about, Red? Because when I said my vows, there was nothing fake about them."

"That's not what I meant." I move toward him, hating the space between us. "It's just that ... I had been drinking and—"

"So help me God," Julian says, "if you tell me you were too drunk to remember marrying me ..."

"No! No." I shake my head. "It's just that in my *slightly* inebriated state, I didn't think about the fact that my dad wasn't here to walk me down the aisle. He's going to be so upset. Not only did he miss me getting married, but it looks bad ... it looks *reckless*."

"Don't do that," he demands. "Don't take something that was meaningful and turn it into something dirty."

"I'm not! But you can't deny how it'll look to an outsider. I know I said I didn't see myself getting married, but a part of me still fantasized about it. The beautiful venue, the white dress, my fiancé dressed in a sharp tux. My dad would tell me I looked like a princess, and then he'd walk me down the aisle and give me away."

I get choked up, thinking about it. "My mom isn't alive anymore, but my dad is. And ... I don't know." I shrug. "I just didn't imagine myself getting married in the middle of the night in Vegas."

"So, you do regret it," he says softly.

"No." I shake my head and circle my arms around his neck. "I don't regret marrying you, Julian. I love you.

I just need some time to come up with a way to tell my dad that I'm married without sounding like what we did was reckless. That even though we did it in the middle of the night in Vegas, it was still meaningful. Please tell me you understand."

"I get it," he says after several beats. "I won't say anything until you tell me it's okay to do so."

"Thank you."

I lift onto my tippy-toes and kiss the corner of his mouth. Before I can pull back, he fists the back of my wet hair and yanks my face up. He kisses his way down my throat, nipping at my flesh as he does so, sending a shiver racing through my body.

Spinning me around, he pushes me up against the cool marble wall of the shower and slaps my ass, making me yelp in a mixture of pleasure and pain.

"I might not be able to claim you as my wife in public," he murmurs against my ear. "But make no fucking mistake ... you. Are. Mine. Mine to kiss." He turns my face and claims my mouth with a fierceness and passion that makes the rest of the world disappear. "Mine to touch." He reaches around and palms one of my breasts roughly as his other hand slides down my body and cups my pussy. "And mine to fuck."

He parts my folds and circles his thumb around my clit in the perfect way he knows I like that will get me off quickly. I've never been with a man who paid so close attention to everything about me. My likes, dislikes. Julian is not only a selfless lover, but he's also like that in every aspect regarding me. He knows what I prefer to drink, what my favorite foods are. He noticed quickly that I need to read to fall asleep, and if I leave my book somewhere, he puts it on the nightstand before bed.

I always thought I was better off alone, without the complications, so I could focus on what was important—my future. But now, I realize that I didn't know any better. Like a child who's never been loved, they don't know to miss the love. I didn't know what I was missing out on, having someone to talk to about my day, share my ups and downs with. Getting off isn't just about quickly finding my release anymore. It's about connecting with someone on a deeper, more intimate level.

My orgasm rips through me, and I shudder as waves of pleasure course through my body. Julian only waits long enough for me to ride it out before he turns me back around, lifts me against the wall, and plunges into me. My body is sensitive from my orgasm, and I scream out in pleasure as he fucks me fast and hard, as if he needs to remind both of us that I am his.

When I come again, it's around his cock, screaming his name in pure ecstasy as he repeatedly says, "*You are mine*," punctuating it with every thrust.

I assume he's going to come inside me, so I'm confused when he pulls out and sets me on my feet. "Show me that you're mine," he says, stroking his cock.

It only takes me a second to understand what he wants, and I drop to my knees, taking over stroking him.

"I'm yours," I tell him, our eyes locked in a heated stare. "I'm all fucking yours."

I part my lips and suck gently on the head, and he explodes all over my face. I could have easily opened my mouth and swallowed it down, but I know what Julian wanted—to claim me.

And he proves that when he stares down at the ribbons of cum all over me, his gaze burning with molten desire. He swipes a finger through the stickiness and drags it over to my lips, painting them like his cum is lipstick.

I press a kiss to the pad of his finger, then bite down on it playfully, and he smirks mischievously, his tell-tale sign that he wants to be inside me.

"Not happening," I tell him, standing and kissing him quickly before moving around him to rinse off. "We have too much to do today to spend it in the shower."

"Fine," he mutters. "But when we get back, I'm taking you away. Somewhere *private*, where I can stay inside your perfect cunt for days."

"Only on one condition ..." I lean in and cup the side of his face. "You also fuck my other holes."

"Jesus, Red," he groans. "You can't say shit like that after telling me I'm not allowed to be inside you." He glances down at his growing erection. "Now, I'm going to be thinking about fucking your ass all day."

The thought has me squirming in my spot, and like the sex fiend my husband has turned me into, I reach out and grasp his shaft.

"Maybe we have time for one more round of sex."

"Mine," he growls, grabbing the side of my face. "All fucking mine."

Twenty-Six

JULIAN

"Welcome back!" Samuel hugs his daughter and then me.

We arrived home from Vegas late last night, and Samuel requested a meeting with us this morning, so with less than a few hours of sleep, we dragged ourselves into work.

"Everyone's talking about the event," he says, sitting across from me and Ana in the conference room. "The feedback is exceptional, and the numbers speak for themselves."

As he pulls up the data, Josie drops off breakfast and coffee.

Ana grabs a coffee and inhales it like an addict, moaning like it's the best thing she's ever tasted.

When our eyes meet, I quirk a brow, and she smirks, knowing exactly what she's doing to me. My wife is a sexy minx.

We spend the next thirty minutes going over the data, and it's safe to say this event was successful and we'll be looking to do more collabs like this in the future.

Before Samuel concludes, he asks if there's anything either of us wants to share, so I use this opportunity to let him know about the deal I signed.

"The Houston Flyers have signed on for Kingston to be their official sponsor this season."

"Nicely done," Samuel says with a nod. "I didn't even know you were working on that."

"It kind of fell into my lap," I admit, "and I didn't want to say anything until I knew for sure since they'd yet to have a liquor company as a sponsor. But the contracts were signed this morning, and our team will be moving forward with the Flyers marketing team to ensure everything is ready to go when the season starts in October."

"Good job, son." Samuel grins proudly. "I can't wait to hear more about it later." He glances from me to Ana. "Anything else?"

"The day care is moving forward," Ana says. "I reached out to a woman named Iris—who owns a childcare agency that specializes in partnering with employee-sponsored childcare programs—to get the ball rolling. We went over the specifics and created a plan. If all goes well, the childcare should be up and running in late spring."

"So much good is happening here," Samuel says. "It saddens me to think about retiring at the end of the year, but I know that Kingston will thrive, no matter who takes my place." He clears his throat. "Which leads me to your next task." He glances from Ana to me. "You guys did so well working on the club event together. I'd like you to work together again to come up with a plan for a corporate event."

"If you keep having us work together, how will you determine who should be the CEO?" Ana asks.

"Working together is a big part of running a company," Samuel says with a shrug, not elaborating any further. "I'd like for it to be held at the end of the month. Something everyone can enjoy and bring their families to. Once you have an idea, let me know, and we'll schedule a meeting."

He closes his laptop and stands. "I'm proud of the way you both have stepped up," he says sincerely. "A couple of months ago, I was worried about leaving, but you've shown me that Kingston will be in good hands."

With a soft smile to Ana and me, he makes his exit, leaving us alone.

"So, what are your thoughts?" I ask.

"I don't know. He seemed off, didn't he?"

I was referring to the corporate event idea, but now that she brings it up ...

"I think he's just getting emotional. This company has been his life for years, and in a few months, he'll be stepping back and letting someone else be in charge. Sure, I handle most of the day-to-day stuff now, but he'll no longer have a title. It's probably starting to feel real."

"Yeah," she says with a nod. "You're probably right. Any ideas for the corporate event?"

"Not off the top of my head. I have a few things to take care of, and then I'll focus on that. Want to discuss it over lunch?"

"Only if lunch involves you eating me," she says with a smirk.

"You're horny this morning." I drag her rolling chair closer to me. "Not that I'm complaining, but it's not like you to instigate sex in the office at nine in the morning." I tuck a hair that's fallen out of her bun behind her ear.

"Well, maybe that's a sign my husband needs to step up and satisfy me," she says haughtily.

I throw my head back with a laugh. "The sex on the plane and in the shower last night and again this morning wasn't enough?"

"Look, if you can't keep up ..."

"You know damn well I can," I growl, leaning in so our mouths are only inches from each other. "I'll see you at noon. I'll order lunch, and you bring the dessert." I peck her lips. "And by dessert, I mean your sweet pussy."

"A PICNIC."

"Lame."

"A beach day," Ana volleys.

"Double lame."

She glares at me. "Okay, what's your amazing idea?"

She brings her chopsticks to her pouty lips and pops a piece of sushi into her mouth, and for a second, I'm so distracted by her that I forget what we're talking about.

"Is it time for dessert yet?"

She rolls her eyes. "Sure, as soon as you agree that a picnic or a beach day is perfect for the corporate event."

"Anastasia Parker," I mock. "Did you just offer me sex in exchange for me agreeing to go along with your idea? Tsk-tsk," I chide. "That's not very legal."

"One, it's Anastasia Kingston-Webb. And two—"

Before she can finish her sentence, I have her thrown over my shoulder, and I'm walking her over to the couch. When I drop her onto her back, she bounces slightly.

"Julian!"

"What's your last name?" I ask, caging her in with my arms while I pin her hips with my own.

"I haven't changed it yet," she says, squirming under me.

My wife might have an exterior as hard as a concrete wall, but all it takes is me offering up my cock, and she turns into a puddle of liquid.

"I don't give a fuck," I tell her, reaching between us. Today, she's wearing a flowy dress that buttons down the front, giving me easy access. "What's your last name?"

She shoots a defying glare at me, and I push her tiny excuse for underwear aside and thrust two fingers inside her.

"You gonna tell me?" I ask, pumping them in and out of her while my thumb massages her clit.

"Kingston," she gasps, playing games.

My fingers go deeper, harder, and she moans, only a few strokes away from detonating.

"Try again," I warn. "And if you answer wrong this time, I'm going to stop."

Her eyes widen at the thought, and I pretend like I'm going to make good on my threat.

"Don't you dare," she breathes. "I'm so close."

"What's your last name?"

I apply pressure to her clit, and she screams, "Parker," as she comes all over my fingers and hand, her entire body shaking in pleasure.

"Damn right it is."

I pull my fingers out and make a show of licking her juices off them. She's the perfect mix of sweet and sour, and if I could survive off her pussy, I'd eat her for every meal.

"I don't give a fuck that you want to keep this marriage a secret. Every single part of you belongs to me, including your last name. Understood?"

"You sound like a caveman," she sasses. "Feminists all over the world are rioting in protest."

"If it makes any difference," I tell her, leaning over and licking her lips, "I'm yours just as much as you're mine."

"Yeah, yeah," she says, reaching down and pulling my cock out of my pants. "How about you stop talking and start showing me just how much you're mine?"

And because I need to make up for the fact that I won't be taking her last name, I show her how much she owns me—twice.

"A BASEBALL GAME," I SAY AS ANA AND I LIE ON THE couch, both of us sweaty and the room smelling like straight-up sex. Before her, I never would've had sex in my office, but with her, I lose all common sense.

"Lame," she says, throwing my answer back at me.

"No, it's not." I shift so she's draped over me and I can look at her. "Have you ever been?"

"No," she says in a way that sounds like I offended her.

"Then, you can't judge. There's a reason why it's America's favorite pastime. It's family friendly. There're tons of food, drinks, and memorabilia with the best entertainment."

When she gives a look that says she's not buying what I'm selling, I come up with an idea.

"How about this? I'll take you to a baseball game, and if you still think it's lame afterward, we'll go with one of your ideas."

"Deal."

Twenty-Seven

ANASTASIA

"OH MY GOD, IT'S SO HOT." I TRY TO FAN MY FACE with the stupid foam finger Julian bought me when we arrived at the baseball stadium, but with the humidity, all I'm doing is fanning more hot air into my face.

When we first arrived, I was starving, so I focused on eating my hot dog—which was surprisingly delicious—and drinking my beer. Now that I'm full, the sun glaring down on us is what has my attention.

"We probably should've gone to a night game," Julian mentions, glancing around. "Follow me."

He stands and takes my hand in his, and I willingly go with him, hoping we're leaving.

I seriously don't know what he was thinking, suggesting a baseball game as a corporate event. Maybe if he wants to punish the employees, this is the way to go.

Instead of heading toward the Exit sign, Julian ascends the stairs until we're under an overhang, and then he walks us halfway across the stadium to a fully shaded area that's up against the wall. It's a bit hard to see from up here, but at least I'm not melting.

"There's, like, nobody here," I point out once we're seated and watching the game. "How do they even bring in any money?"

Julian chuckles. "They play a hundred sixty-two games. People watch them on TV, and the broadcasting rights make them money. Plus, the sponsorships and merch."

"A hundred sixty-two games?" I gasp. "Those poor guys."

I can barely sit through one game. I can't imagine having to play damn near two hundred.

"It's just because you don't understand the game," Julian says.

He goes into explaining the positions and who the players are. He knows so much about sports, and despite my not giving a crap about the sport or what's going on, it's cute to listen to how excited he gets when he tells me how he met the team once and got several of their autographs.

Instead of paying attention to the boring game, I find myself watching my husband. Holy shit, I'm married. It's still crazy to believe that we went from being fake engaged to getting married.

But I meant what I told him. I don't regret it. Every day, I fall harder for Julian. His work ethic, his patience. He's such a good man. He's easy to talk to and sweet. And then there's the chemistry between us.

The harder I fall, the more I want him. The past week, I've been so damn horny that I have to wonder how I went so long without having sex on the regular. But maybe it's because even though I preferred the random hookups without any strings attached, getting to know Julian is a lot of why I want him the way I do.

And it's not just the sex. As we sit here and he talks about something he loves, I realize I could listen to him for hours. I don't care about baseball in the slightest, but I love listening to Julian talk.

He says something and glances at me with a smile, and I find myself smiling back. That's what he does to me—makes me forget that anybody but us exists. The entire world around us could be burning to the ground, and my focus would only be on him.

He leans down and presses his lips to mine in what is supposed to be a quick kiss. Only I'm craving more, so when he goes to pull back, I slide my tongue into his mouth, not wanting the kiss to end. He tastes like the perfect mixture of sweet and bitter from having just taken a sip of his beer, and I suck on his tongue, wanting more.

We kiss for several minutes, our tongues stroking and teasing one another. And when kissing him isn't enough to satisfy my need for him, I climb into his lap, deepening our connection.

I'm wearing a floral sundress that's tight on the top and flares loosely on the bottom with a pair of lace panties underneath, so when I settle into Julian's lap, there's only a thin piece of material stopping me from completely feeling his hard length.

I grind against his pelvis, and our kiss becomes desperate, our tongues moving frantically against each other. I'm on top of him, kissing him, but it's not enough. I always want more. Crave more.

"I want you," I murmur against his mouth.

We must be on the same page because as I shift back slightly, prepared to pull his cock out, he quickly undoes the button and zipper, exposing one of my favorite parts of him.

He's hard and ready, and I waste no time, shoving my panties to the side and lifting so I can lower myself onto him. I'm wet, but not foreplay wet, so he feels bigger as my pussy stretches to accommodate every inch of him.

"Fuck yeah, baby. Ride my cock," he says as his hand twists in my hair and he brings my face back to his.

His lips part mine, and his tongue sinks inside, his skilled mouth devouring mine as I ride him, slow yet deep.

When my climax rockets through me, turning my legs into jelly, Julian breaks our kiss and takes over, driving into me from the bottom with quick, erratic thrusts that stop when he finds his own release.

With my face nuzzled into his neck, I'm working on catching my breath when the sound of people clapping remind me that we're at a baseball game.

Oh shit. We're at a baseball game, and my husband's cock is inside of me.

"You okay?" he asks with a chuckle.

"Yeah," I squeak. "Just wondering how I'm going to get up without your cum dripping down the inside of my thighs."

"You trying to get fucked again?" he growls like the caveman he is.

"Julian, focus."

"I have napkins in my pocket." He lifts and sets me on the chair next to him in one fluid motion, somehow tucking himself back into his pants, and then pulls out a bunch of napkins.

I try to wipe myself the best I can without looking like a perve.

I know. I know. We just fucked in public. That ship has sailed.

But in my defense, when his dick is involved, I can't think clearly. It's like I have dick brain.

I giggle at my joke, and he glances at me like I've lost my shit.

"You ready?" he asks.

"Yep."

We stop at the restroom so we can clean up a little better and then head out. On our way to the car, a weird feeling comes over me, like someone is watching us, but when I look around, I don't see anyone, so I chalk it up to my brain being foggy from just having had some amazing sex.

Only the next morning, when we walk into the office, I realize I wasn't wrong. Someone was watching us. And they got a whole lot more than just us walking to the car.

"BOTH OF YOU, IN MY OFFICE NOW," DAD SAYS, HIS tone reminding me of when I was a teenager and did something that disappointed him.

Julian presses his hand to my back in a comforting gesture, and we follow my dad into his office.

He closes the door behind us, and when we turn around, the fury in his eyes has me taking a hesitant step backward. It's been years since I've been on the other end of my dad's wrath. And even though I'm a grown woman, I find myself slinking closer to Julian for comfort.

"What the hell were you doing at a baseball game in Houston?" Dad demands, referring to the baseball game we went to.

What? That's what he's asking about?

"Julian wanted to do the corporate event there, so he dragged me to watch a game." I roll my eyes playfully despite the current tension in the room. "It's safe to say, we won't be doing it at—"

"That's not what I'm talking about!" Dad barks, making me jump back.

I stumble slightly, but Julian catches me before I land on my ass.

"This is what I'm talking about." Dad walks over to his desk, clicks his mouse a few times, and then swivels his computer monitor around.

It takes me a second to comprehend what we're looking at, for my brain to catch up with what it's seeing. But once I do, I gasp in shock and embarrassment.

There's no way ...

It can't be ...

My mind must be playing tricks on me ...

I blink several times, but the video is still there in color—me riding Julian at the baseball game. You can't see anything, thanks to my dress being fanned out around us, but between us kissing and my body moving up and down, it's obvious what's happening.

Without waiting for the video to finish, my dad hits a button on his computer that blacks out the screen.

"Where did you get that?" Julian says calmly while I freak the hell out because, holy shit, we're on video, having sex!

"It's all over the internet," Dad says. "I have PR working to do damage control, but there's only so much they can do. This is not the image I was talking about when we discussed the future of Kingston. It's bad enough two of my employees are in the video, but for it to be my daughter and the COO? The calls have already started coming in from our business associates."

His gaze meets mine. "And to find out you got married behind my back in Vegas from a *tabloid* ..." His features morph from angry to hurt, and my heart sinks.

"It's like you're a teenager all over again, acting reckless and making dumb decisions without thinking. You're not a child anymore, Anastasia. And, Julian ..." He shakes his head. "I expected better than this from you."

"Samuel," Julian says at the same time I say, "Dad, listen ..."

"I've heard enough," he says, those three words eliciting memories from when I was younger.

Every time I messed up and tried to explain. When I disappointed him and he'd give me a lecture without letting me speak my side. Memory after memory flits through my head until it becomes too much, and I snap.

"No, you haven't heard anything from *me*," I choke out. "You saw the video, and you read the tabloids, but you didn't hear from me or Julian. You always do this!" I cry. "I mess up, and you don't listen to me. But you mess up, and I'm supposed to listen, right? You spent years after Mom's death begging me to listen to you! Now, please, listen to me!"

Dad stares at me in shock for several moments before he nods and takes a seat. "Okay, talk."

"Thank you," I breathe.

Taking Julian's hand in mine, I walk us over to the visitor chairs across from my dad and sit.

"I've done a lot of dumb things in my life, made many poor decisions, but being with Julian isn't one of them," I begin. "I know we messed up, and I'll do whatever you need to make it right, and I know Julian will, too, because he loves you and cares about this company.

"But instead of judging, try to remember what it's like to be young and in love. We didn't set out to hurt anyone, especially this company. I know I'm your employee, but I'm also your daughter. And for the first time in my life, I'm in love." I glance at Julian, who smiles softly at me. "Please, stop thinking like a business owner for one second and think like a dad," I say, looking back at my dad.

He stares at Julian and me for several seconds, and I have no clue what he's going to do or say, but then he sighs and says, "You're both going to release an apology statement that our PR team draws up. It helps that you're married, so we can spin it to say that it wasn't simply a hookup. In the future, I expect you both to keep your personal lives private. Understood?"

Dad raises a brow, and we both nod.

"And as for the secret marriage, I'm not going to lie and say it didn't hurt to learn I wasn't in the know, but I guess I deserve that after everything that's happened."

"No," I tell him, shaking my head. "I promise, it wasn't like that."

Dad nods. "All right, well, there's a lot to do, so go ahead and get to work, and PR will be in touch soon."

And just like that, we've been dismissed.

"And, Anastasia?"

"Yeah?" I say, stopping in my tracks by the door.

"I'm proud of you. Regardless of the mistakes you make, I'm still proud of everything you've accomplished, and I know your mother would be too."

Twenty-Eight

JULIAN

"What do we do for the corporate event now?" Ana asks once we're in my office. "Because we're sure as hell not having it at a baseball game."

"We could always do football," I deadpan.

"Hell no!" she shrieks, making me laugh.

"I'm just kidding."

"Too soon." She glares.

"I guess a company picnic it is."

"Good choice."

"I wonder if I can get a copy of that video," I say, typing our names into the search engine.

"What for?" she hisses.

"Did you see that small clip of you riding my cock?" I smirk. "If it hasn't been taken down yet, that video is going into my spank bank."

"It's not too late to file for an annulment," Ana says, coming around the desk and leaning over me to swat my hands away from the keyboard.

I drag her into my lap and twist her so she's facing me. "You wouldn't dare," I warn, fisting the back of her hair. "Besides, I saw the way you squirmed when your dad showed us the video." I pull her head toward mine. "You were as turned on as I was, watching yourself ride my cock."

Without waiting for her to respond, I kiss her luscious mouth. When I slide my tongue past her parted lips so I can taste her, she sighs into me.

Despite having just got caught on video, fucking my wife, I'm considering taking her on my desk when there's a quick rap on the door, followed by Ryder strolling in, like he always does.

"Jesus," he says with a laugh as Ana shuffles off my lap and stands. "You'd think getting caught fornicating at a baseball game would slow you two down. Guess not."

"You saw it, huh?" I smirk, making Ana glare my way.

"I'm pretty sure everyone has," Ryder says with a chuckle.

"I should probably get to work," Ana mutters, walking toward the door.

"Actually, I'm glad I caught you both," Ryder says. "Nora has been hounding me to get out. She's bored at home." He rolls his eyes, and I refrain from saying what I'm thinking—maybe her lazy ass should get a job. "She wants to hang out with other adults, and the last thing I want is to go out with her friends."

"No." I shake my head, knowing where this is going.

"C'mon, please," Ryder begs, giving Ana the saddest puppy-dog eyes.

"No," I insist. "That woman is the literal devil."

"We'd love to," Ana says. "How about Friday night? We don't have any plans."

"That would be great. Thanks." Ryder grins at her. "How about Lush? She's been wanting to try the place out."

"I'll get us reservations," I drawl.

"Thank you. I owe you."

"Big time," I agree.

Ryder leaves, closing the door behind him, and I walk over to Ana.

With her back to me, I rest my hands on her hips and my chin on her shoulder. "Now, where were we?"

"We are not having sex anywhere but in our house for the foreseeable future," she says, turning around.

"Where's the fun in that?"

I waggle my brows, and she playfully smacks my chest.

"Not happening." She presses a quick kiss to my lips and then backs up. "I'm going to get started on the details for the company picnic. I'll see you later."

Once she's gone, I go about researching a wedding planner. My wife wants a real wedding, so she's going to get one that she'll never forget.

"I THINK I'M GOING TO GO AWAY FOR A FEW DAYS."

I glance up from my phone and set it down, finding Ana standing in front of me.

"You mean, *we're* going to go away for a few days?" I correct.

"No." She shakes her head. "I meant me."

She swallows thickly, and I see it in her features that she's trying to push me away.

It's been a long week, dealing with the fallout from the baseball-game footage. Kingston's attorneys were able to get it taken down, but not before it went viral on social media. Our IT department has been working around the clock to get them removed, but it will never happen. Once something like that is out in the world, there's no wiping it away completely.

And with every video that's found and posted and commented on, she retreats into her shell a little more.

"See, that's where you're wrong."

I lock the door behind her and then guide us over to the couch.

When I sit, I expect her to cuddle into my side, like she always does, but instead, she places herself on the other side, keeping her distance.

"I just think I need some space," she whispers.

"No," I argue, reaching across the couch and pulling her into my arms so she's sitting across my lap. "What you need is to realize that you're not in this alone. And while I get you running after your mom passed away, you're not running now."

She buries her face in my neck and sniffles, and I wrap my arms around her as she cries quietly in my arms.

While guys get a slap on the back for getting caught in a sex-tape scandal, women don't have it as easy, and I've heard the way people are whispering about Ana behind her back. When we walk through the office together, people stare and judge. I've had to tell several employees to close their mouths when I caught them making comments.

"I was thinking that maybe I should quit." She sniffles softly. "But who else is going to hire me after that video?"

"It's going to pass," I promise her, lifting her chin to look up at me. "I know it's hard right now, but you're stronger than this. You don't quit, Red. You keep your chin up and say *fuck you* to anyone who tries to look down on you."

"Easier said than done," she mumbles, dropping her head back down to my shoulder and snuggling closer. "Even my dad is being weird. I asked him to have lunch with me today since it's Wednesday, and he told me he was too busy."

"In his defense, he rescheduled a meeting we had for today because he said he had an appointment and wouldn't be in."

"Really?" She lifts her head. "Did he say why?"

"No, but I don't think he's blowing you off."

"Maybe," she says noncommittally. "I still think I should go away. Out of sight, out of mind and all that."

"And as I said, you're not going anywhere without me. We're in this together. Where do you want to go?"

"I don't know." She shrugs, still pouting. "It's beautiful in Florida this time of year."

I chuckle at how adorable she is. To everyone else, she's a strong, stubborn badass, but with me, she lets that shield down and shows me her vulnerable side. And it makes me love her even more.

"We have the double date on Friday night," I remind her, making her groan. "But we could leave Saturday morning."

"And take a couple of days off?" she says hopefully. "Make it a long weekend?"

"We can do that."

I've barely taken any days off in years. Nobody will blink an eye at me actually using a few personal days.

"Thank you," she murmurs, reaching up and kissing the corner of my jaw. "I've been feeling so blah this week. I think I just need a weekend away to regroup."

"Hey," I say, palming her cheek. "It's all going to be okay." I lean down and kiss the tip of her nose, and her lashes flutter shut. "In a few months, nobody is even going to remember what happened."

"I hope you're right," she says with a sigh.

We sit in silence for a few minutes, and I'm about to ask if she wants to order in lunch when I hear a soft snore coming from her. She's fallen asleep.

Not wanting to wake her up, I pull my phone out and search for resorts in Florida. I find one on the beach with a gorgeous view, a kick-ass pool, and a spa that I know she'll love.

After getting it booked, I text Samuel to make sure he's okay if I use the company jet. When he replies, he asks if everything is okay.

ME

People are giving Ana shit about the video. She wants to go away, so I booked us a resort in Fort Lauderdale.

SAMUEL

She's not going to quit, is she?

I glance down at my strong, determined wife. She might be down now, but soon, she'll be back up, giving everyone hell again. A few months ago, I would've been hoping for her to quit, but things have changed, and I can't imagine my life without her.

ME

We won't let her. When we get back, I need to talk to you.

SAMUEL

You got it. Take care of my little girl.

ME

Always.

Twenty-Nine

ANASTASIA

"Jesus, you look like walking sin, dressed like that."

Julian strolls into our bedroom, dressed in a pair of black dress pants and a crisp white button-down shirt, tie loose and waiting to be tied. His eyes are filled with unadulterated lust as he takes in my little red halter dress that crisscrosses over my breasts, leaving my skin on display. The dress is short and tight, and I feel sexy in it.

"Is it new?" he asks, stepping over to me and running his fingertip along my exposed flesh just below my breast.

"Yep, I went emotional shopping this morning," I admit.

With the whispers still running rampant, I took personal days yesterday and today. Yesterday, I sulked in bed, crying on and off all day while searching for the video of us and sending each one I found to IT so they could request for them to be taken down.

Julian came home with dinner and pretended like I didn't look like an emotional train wreck while we ate and then spent the rest of the evening watching a movie I don't even remember.

This morning, when I woke up, I remembered we had the double date tonight and then we'd be leaving for Fort Lauderdale in the morning, so I decided some shopping was in order.

"I don't like that you've been hiding out," he says, sliding his hand around to my backside and squeezing. "But I'm completely on board with this dress."

"If you like this dress, you should see the outfits and lingerie I bought for this weekend."

I take the hand that's not grabbing my ass and glide it under my dress to my lace panties. "These are brand-new."

"You can't do shit like this before we're due to leave for dinner," he murmurs, making no effort to remove his hand from my panties. "I'm going to be hard, thinking about you the entire meal."

"Well, we wouldn't want that, now would we?" I taunt, rubbing his already-forming erection.

"Red," he groans. "We're going to be late."

"Not if we hurry."

I unbutton and unzip his pants and pull his hard length out, then drop to my knees and take him in my mouth. The head is soft, and as I glide my lips along his shaft, taking him down my throat, I moan around him, loving how good he smells and tastes since he just got out of the shower.

I bob my head up and down, working his cock over while I gently fondle his balls, just how he likes it. When I glance up through my lashes, I catch him staring down at me in awe.

"So fucking perfect," he murmurs, lovingly stroking my cheek while I fuck him with my mouth.

I never thought I would be this woman—on her knees for a man—but Julian doesn't treat me like I'm less than him. He sees me as his equal, his partner, in and out of the bedroom.

Falling in love wasn't what was supposed to happen when I came here, but he's quickly come to mean so much to me. I wasn't expecting him, but now, I can't imagine not having him.

"Baby, I'm going to come," he mutters, gently pulling my face off his cock. "Come here."

He helps me to my feet and then lifts me onto the dresser.

I pull my dress up to my hips so it doesn't rip, and then he spreads my legs.

He drops to his knees and tugs my panties down my thighs.

"These are drenched," he says, fisting them and making a show of inhaling the scent.

He tosses them to the side and opens my legs so he can lick up my center. I'm sensitive to his touch, and I damn near come on the spot. With a chuckle, he sucks on my clit, and within seconds, I'm climaxing all over his tongue.

He gives my pussy an open-mouthed kiss, then stands and pulls my legs to the edge. Without giving me a chance to come down from my orgasm, he thrusts into me, filling me to the hilt.

Without holding back, he fucks me like he's claiming me all over again. His hand palms my cheek, and his mouth comes down on mine, kissing me with so much passion that I get lost in everything that is Julian Parker. The world around us no longer exists. The rumors and whispers have disappeared. And for this moment, it's just us, making love, everything and everyone else be damned.

His hand that was holding my face glides down my neck, and he breaks the kiss, wrapping his fingers around my throat.

"You're mine," he murmurs, fucking me deep and hard with steady thrusts. "Till death do us part."

He slides his hand down to my breast and pinches my nipple through the material. With my body being hypersensitive, it's enough to send me over the precipice. I clench around Julian's cock, and he falls over the edge with me.

"Thank you," I murmur as we stay connected, both of us catching our breath.

"For sex?" He smirks. "Baby, you never have to thank me for fucking my wife."

"No," I say with a laugh. "For not letting me run and for being patient with me the past few days. I don't know what's going on with me, but this whole video thing has really hit me hard. I feel so all over the place."

"I've got you," he says. "Whatever happens, we're in it together."

He presses a soft kiss to my lips and then pulls out, quickly grabbing a shirt from nearby to catch his cum that's slowly leaking out of me.

He helps me off the dresser, and then we both head to the bathroom to get cleaned up.

We're late to meet Nora and Ryder for dinner, but as I told Julian, it was well worth it.

"Oh God, Ryder, must you order something so fishy?" Nora whines for what feels like the millionth time tonight.

First, she complained it was too hot in here—apparently pregnant women run warm. Then, she asked to be moved because the gentleman sitting too close to us had cologne that made her want to throw up. Once we were seated again, she complained that the music was too loud—she's had horrible headaches throughout the pregnancy, and she isn't allowed to take anything strong. Now, the fish Ryder ordered is too fishy.

I'm about to say something to change the subject when I get a whiff of Ryder's salmon and find myself choking from the smell as well.

I cough a few times to try to get a handle on it, but when it feels like I'm going to throw up, I quickly excuse myself to use the restroom, where I barely make it in time to throw up everything in my stomach.

After rinsing out my mouth and washing my hands, I head out of the restroom and run straight into Julian.

"You okay?" he asks, looking concerned.

"Yeah, I don't know what's wrong with me," I say honestly. "Maybe I'm coming down with something."

"Does your throat hurt? Do you feel weak?" He presses the back of his hand to my forehead. "You don't feel warm."

"I don't feel sick. I think it's just all the stress from this week." I shrug, unsure how to explain it. "It's messing with my body."

"Good thing we're going away," he says, wrapping an arm around me and pressing a kiss on my temple.

When we return to the table, Ryder's fish is gone, and he and Nora are arguing under their breaths.

"Sorry about that," I say, sitting back down. "I've been feeling weird all week."

"Try feeling weird for nine months," Nora laments.

"It's only been a few months," Ryder mutters under his breath.

"Do you have any idea what it feels like to feel nauseous twenty-four/seven?" Nora cries. "To have aching breasts and a sore body and be emotional all the damn time?"

Tears fill her eyes, and I can't help but feel bad for her. It's clear she's struggling with being pregnant—even if there's a chance that she did this to herself.

"That sounds horrible," I tell her, trying to be compassionate while thanking the birth-control gods that I'm protected.

"It is," she mutters through a sniffle. "And I still have, like, a million more months to go."

"Well, on the bright side," I say, stifling down my laughter at her dramatics, "at the end of all that pain and suffering, you'll have a beautiful, healthy baby."

I smile at Nora, who nods in agreement, while Ryder sighs in what looks like defeat.

"We should totally get together sometime," Nora suggests a little while later while we eat our dessert.

Thankfully, the rest of the meal was uneventful, and without having anything to complain about, Nora has been almost pleasant. But that sure as hell doesn't mean I want to spend time with her.

"Oh," I say, trying to come up with something to say. "I'm so busy with work ..."

"But not for long, right?" she inquires. "You guys are married now."

"Um, yeah, we're married," I say slowly, confused by her statement. "But I still have every intention of working. As a matter of fact, if things go my way, my husband will be working for me soon enough."

I wink playfully at Julian, and he chuckles.

"What do you mean?" Nora asks.

"We're both going for the CEO position," I explain. "My dad is retiring, and at the end of the year, he's going to select one of us to replace him."

Nora scrunches her nose up like she smells something gross. "Why would you want to be the CEO? Aren't you worth millions?"

"Nora," Ryder hisses.

"What?" she says innocently. "I just don't get it. Why would you want to emasculate your husband by trying to take his job when you don't even have to work?"

"Because Ana is just as capable of being the CEO as I am," Julian says, sliding his hand to my thigh and squeezing it. "She's smart and educated, and she knows the business as well as I do. And just because she's a woman who comes from money, it doesn't mean she should be home while I work. My wife is a marketing badass, and nothing about her fighting for the CEO position is emasculating." He looks over at me with heat in his eyes. "It's a fucking turn-on."

And that right there is why I love my husband.

"What would it take to convince you to move here?" I ask Julian, my eyes closed as we lie out in lounge chairs that are covered by large umbrellas, keeping the direct sun off us, but allowing us to enjoy the South Florida heat in September.

"Probably not much," he says, running a hand up my thigh despite there being dozens of people around.

I've learned that my husband doesn't give a shit about public displays of affection. He loves to touch me and doesn't care where we are or who we're with.

"But we both know you'd be bored in about two seconds," he adds with a chuckle.

I pop a lid open and mock glare even though he's not wrong. We've been in Fort Lauderdale for three days, and I barely made it the first day before I was doing work on my laptop for a marketing campaign I had been asked to look into. I love my job, and Julian was right when he said I'd get past everything that'd happened.

A few days ago, one of the managers got caught on the security camera, hooking up with a college intern, and everyone has been gossiping about it. Julian thinks once we return, no one will even remember what happened between us. I hope he's right.

"It's getting hot," he murmurs. "What do you say we go upstairs to cool off and take a nap?"

Since I know that's code for Julian wanting to fuck me on our private balcony, I hop up, but when I do, the world around me slightly spins. Since I haven't drunk any alcohol, it's not from being drunk, which makes me think it's …

"Red, you good?" Julian asks, glancing at me with concern.

"Yeah, just got up too quickly."

I laugh it off, throwing on my bathing suit cover-up and sliding on my flip-flops.

The moment we're inside and the door is closed, Julian backs me against the wall and attacks my mouth. One hand cradles my face, and the other comes up to massage my breast. I wince in pain before I can stop myself, and because he has his eyes open, he notices.

"Was I too rough?" he asks, his brows dipping in concern.

"No." I shake my head, not wanting to have this conversation with him—hell, I'm not ready to have this conversation with myself yet. "I was just thrown off."

I pull him back to me and kiss him, knowing it will get him back on course.

But the entire time we make love, I can't help thinking about what Nora said at dinner. *Do you have any idea what it feels like to feel nauseous twenty-four/seven? To have aching breasts and a sore body and be emotional all the damn time?*

It makes no sense. I'm on birth control. I've had the IUD for the past two years.

Julian comes, but the second he does, he notices that I didn't.

"What's going on with you?" he asks.

"Nothing, I'm just in my own head. I have a lot on my mind."

"Anything you want to talk about?"

"Not right now," I tell him truthfully.

"Okay, well, my wife isn't going without an orgasm, so it looks like I'm going to have to work twice as hard to get you out of your head so your only thought is coming all over my mouth and fingers."

And with that promise, he spends the next half hour making me come not once, but twice. And for a brief time, he does in fact get me out of my head.

Until the high wears off, and while he's sleeping, I go to the bathroom and feel for the strings that should be between my legs but are missing.

And then I spend the next hour researching doctors in our area so that I can make an appointment when we get home to confirm what I'm almost positive I already know … I'm pregnant.

Thirty

ANASTASIA

"The pregnancy test came back positive."

"Blood work shows high levels of hCG."

"The IUD fell out."

"It rarely happens, but it's possible."

Dr. Bowen's words play on repeat in my head as I lie on the medical table and she pushes a wand into me to do a transvaginal ultrasound to confirm what all signs point to—I'm pregnant.

She clicks around on the computer and then turns the volume up. And like in every movie and book with a plot twist of an unexpected pregnancy, I hear the whooshing of my baby's heartbeat.

She walks me through everything on the screen while I try my best not to cry. I'm due in May. The heartbeat is strong. It's recommended I start taking prenatal vitamins. I need to schedule my next appointment.

As I walk out of the doctor's office, I'm so lost in my head that I don't see the car coming around the corner as I step into the street.

He honks, and I jump.

I'm physically okay, but mentally … I drop onto the edge of the curb and sob.

I'm pregnant. This isn't what was supposed to happen. I was supposed to become CEO of Kingston. Prove to my dad that I'm capable of running the company.

Yet I'm pregnant. I glance down at the ultrasound picture, and my heart swells because despite this being unexpected, I already love the baby growing in my belly.

Which sucks because I can't have both the company and the family. My dad tried that, and look how it turned out. And I can't become my dad. I refuse to.

But also, Julian is so much like my dad, so what will that mean for us? Will I become my mom and he, my dad? Will we grow apart while I beg for attention? Will our child crave his love and affection, only to be given breadcrumbs of what they deserve?

While I'm sitting on the curb, crying, wondering what I'm going to do, a text comes in from Julian's mom, Helen, confirming dinner tonight.

We haven't seen them since the barbecue, so when she reached out, inviting us to dinner, we, of course, said yes. Now, I'm regretting it. Hanging out with the woman who resembles Mary Poppins, Martha Stewart, and Paula Deen is not at the top of my list of things I want to do right now.

Since the day is almost over, instead of going back to work, I head home and take a nap. I wake up several hours later to Julian asking if I'm feeling okay and if we should cancel dinner.

"I'm okay," I tell him, sitting up. "Just give me ten minutes to freshen up."

WHEN WE ARRIVE AT HIS PARENTS' PLACE, I TAKE IN the small but homey-looking house. The front yard is neatly trimmed, and a flower bed with blooming flowers wraps around the house. On the porch are two wooden rocking chairs that I can imagine Helen and Frank rocking in while having their morning coffee.

The inside is even warmer. The walls are filled with family pictures from holidays and vacations. The furniture is clean but well lived in. Unlike the home I grew up in, which screamed wealth and opulence, this home screams love and family.

Helen wraps me in a motherly hug, and I get choked up, missing my mom like crazy—wishing she were here to confide in. She probably wouldn't have the answers I'm looking for since she died trying to figure out her love life, but at least she would be here to support me.

"While the guys watch the game, do you want to help me make Julian's favorite dish?" she offers, zero judgment in her tone.

I nod because it'll probably be good to learn how to cook something, and she's the only person I know who can help me.

"Mom, Ana doesn't like to cook," Julian says, trying to get me out of it.

"No, it's fine," I tell him. "I'd like to learn how to make your favorite dish."

He looks at me like I've grown two heads. "Really, babe? You hate sports that much that you'd rather cook?"

"Go away," I say playfully, pushing on his chest.

He grabs my hands and pulls me in, giving me a quick kiss before he disappears out of the kitchen, and I'm left wondering what will happen to us once he finds out about the baby. We've never discussed having a family—well, aside from the time he jokingly said he wouldn't mind having a couple of mini versions of me running around.

It's only been us and the company. I don't even know if he wants kids … oh God. What if he doesn't want kids? He was counting on me to keep us safe, and my stupid IUD failed. It's not my fault, but that doesn't change the fact that he might not see this baby as a good thing.

Will he divorce me and leave me as a single mom? Will I be forced to choose between my husband and my baby?

My hand protectively goes to my flat stomach, knowing there would be no choice. I would choose this baby every time. I shake all the thoughts from my head, refusing to give in to what-ifs. Thinking about them all could drive a sane person crazy.

"I thought mac 'n' cheese was Julian's favorite," I say when I notice all the meat and veggies spread all over the counter.

"He has a few favorites," Helen notes with a wink. "When he's sick, he loves homemade chicken noodle soup—heavy on the noodle, light on the veggies. At barbecues, he loves mac 'n' cheese with a good burger, but his favorite home-cooked meal is lasagna. So, we're making lasagna tonight with a salad."

She washes her hands, so I follow suit.

"Lasagna is actually super easy to make," she says. "The first thing we want to do is make the tomato sauce."

When she pulls out a bunch of spices and sets them next to fresh tomatoes, I immediately know I'm in over my head. This woman doesn't even use tomato sauce out of a jar.

I watch as she adds all the ingredients to a pan, explaining what each one is, as if I'm seriously going to remember this later. Once that's simmering, she goes about cooking the ground beef. When she notices that I haven't said a word in several minutes, nor have I attempted to help, she stops what she's doing and looks at me.

"Ana, are you okay?"

I try to nod, but instead, I shake my head, and then I lose it, right here in my mother-in-law's kitchen.

She pulls her apron off her and envelops me in a hug, and I cry softly in her arms, not wanting to alert Julian that I'm a sobbing mess.

When I've calmed slightly, she sits us at the table and says, "Talk to me, dear."

"I can't cook," I choke out. "I can't cook or clean or do laundry. I mean, I'm smart. I have a degree and a master's, and I can do numbers all day, but I can't even follow along with a simple lasagna recipe while you walk me through it. And the truth is, I don't want to. I hate cooking. I don't find it fun or enjoyable, and I have no desire to do it," I admit, the words flowing out like a therapeutic river.

"Oh, Ana. I didn't mean to upset you."

"It wasn't you." I sniffle. "It's me. I wasn't supposed to be a wife or a mom. I was meant to run numbers, and now ..." I shake my head, not ready to admit that I'm pregnant yet. Julian should be the first person I tell. "I'm not good at this, I don't want to be good at this, and Julian *deserves* to have a wife who's good at this. I'm going to suck at it, and he's going to resent me, and I'll resent him right back, and where will that leave us?"

Helen hands me a tissue, and I wipe my face and blow my nose.

"You don't suck at anything," Helen says kindly. "But regardless, my son is in love with you, and that's not going to change over who cooks and cleans."

"Yeah, maybe," I agree noncommittally as more thoughts fill my head, like, *Who's going to stay home with the baby?*

My mom raised me with very little help from the nannies, and while I didn't mind the nannies, my fondest memories are of the time spent with my mom.

Can I give it all up, everything I've wanted for my future, to be the mom this baby deserves?

And what about Julian? This is exactly what my dad was talking about when he said he wanted to hire a family man. Someone who knows how to balance work and family. Something neither of us knows how to do.

With the flooding of thoughts and questions, I start to cry again, my emotions in overdrive. Helen hugs me tightly, telling me everything will be okay, and once I've gotten myself together, we make dinner. And by we, I mean she makes it, and I watch while we talk about nothing of substance.

By the time dinner is ready, I barely look like I've been crying, yet from the look on Julian's face, I can tell he suspects something is wrong. The way he's in tune with my thoughts and emotions is kind of crazy.

Thankfully, he doesn't comment on it, and we have a nice dinner with delicious lasagna, garlic bread, and salad. After dessert, we say our goodbyes and head home. And when I tell Julian that I'm tired and I'm going to head to bed, he insists on joining me.

As I fall asleep in his arms, I vow to figure this out soon. Julian and I are both so much like my dad, and I can't allow what happened with my parents to happen to us.

Thirty-One

ANASTASIA

"Hey, Josie. Is Julian in his office?"

He's been in back-to-back meetings all day, but I'm hoping to catch him to see about leaving early tonight so we can talk. I've decided that I'm going to tell him about the baby tonight. And then I'm going to tell my dad that I'm taking a step back. Being a mom isn't what I planned for, but now that it's happening, I want to be the best mom I can be. The same way my mom was to me.

"He should be," she says as I stride past her desk and straight toward his office.

His door is slightly ajar, and before I knock to let him know I'm coming in, in case he's in a meeting, I hear my father's voice, halting me in place.

"I know you're just the man for the job," Dad says as I peek in and watch him extend his hand to Julian.

"Thank you," Julian says, shaking his hand.

"Welcome to the family, son."

They hug, and my entire body goes cold.

Dad wasn't supposed to pick a new CEO until December, yet he went behind my back and chose Julian? And he couldn't even tell me first? I know I said I planned to step down, but, damn, it still hurts knowing that my dad really doesn't believe I'm capable of taking his place as CEO.

I knew there was a chance he'd pick Julian, but to be honest, I really didn't believe he would do it. I'm his daughter, his own flesh and blood. I've busted my ass for years, trying to prove myself in the business world.

But I'm not good enough.

And if I'm not even good at what I know, how the hell am I going to be good at what I don't know?

I've failed at business. And now, I'm going to fail at being a wife and a mom.

Without waiting for their meeting to end, I grab my purse from my office and take off. Since we rode in together, I call for a car service to pick me up. It takes a while since we live in a small town, so I use the time to get a drink and cry.

Once I'm home, I eat something since I'm starving and then lie on the couch to watch some mindless television while I wait for Julian to get home.

I must've fallen asleep on the couch because when I awake, it's dark outside, and Julian is standing over me with a look of concern etched on his features.

"I've been calling and texting you all afternoon," he says. "You couldn't let me know you were going home early?"

"Sorry," I mutter, sitting up on the couch. "I overheard you and my dad talking in your office today," I admit. "I guess congratulations are in order."

Julian's eyes widen, telling me he knows exactly what I heard.

"It's for the best. I have news of my own." I reach over to my purse and pull out the ultrasound picture. "Surprise, I'm pregnant."

I hand him the black-and-white image, and he stares at it in shock. I don't blame him since it was a shock to me as well.

"My IUD fell out," I explain. "I'm due in May."

His eyes ascend to meet mine.

"So, it's for the best that my dad picked you to be the CEO since I'll be busy having a baby." I shrug. "I can't do both. Not that it matters since he doesn't think I'm the best fit for the job anyway."

I laugh humorlessly. "Looks like he got what he wanted after all. His daughter barefoot and pregnant at home while my husband runs the business."

Julian opens his mouth to speak, but I'm on a roll so I keep going. "Sorry you got more than what you bargained for. You wanted a fake engagement, and instead, you got a wife and a baby."

Another laugh bubbles out of me, along with a sob. "All I wanted was for my dad to love me, to see that I'm capable of running Kingston. For him to be proud of me. And instead—"

"You did exactly that," my dad says, making me jump in my spot.

I look over, and he's standing in the foyer.

"Dad, what are you doing here?"

"I was outside on the phone," he says.

"When I couldn't get ahold of you, I got worried," Julian adds. "Your dad tried calling and texting, and when you didn't answer, he came with me to look for you. You've been off lately, and we were worried."

"Well, now, you know," I tell them both. "Nothing's wrong. I'm just pregnant, and you're the new CEO of Kingston."

"I think it's time you and I have a conversation," Dad says, coming over to sit next to me on the couch. He pats my leg and smiles sadly at me. "The truth is, I could run Kingston with my eyes closed, but I had no idea what to do with a daughter who wanted my attention."

"I just wanted you to love me," I whisper, emotions clogging my throat.

"I know," he says, his eyes glassy. "You wanted the same thing as your mother, and I thought that was what I was doing. I had been raised in a poor family. We barely had enough food some days to eat three meals. My parents worked so hard to provide, but it was never enough. They were always fighting over money ... or lack thereof.

"When I left my family home and came to Texas, I thought money would equal happiness. I went to school and majored in business and put all my efforts into my schooling. And then I met your mother. She had been raised in a wealthy family, and when I asked her father for his permission to marry her our sophomore year in college, he said, 'I'll give it to you when you can provide for her like a husband should.'"

"I didn't know that," I admit.

"Nobody knew," he confesses. "I left his house that day, even more motivated to make something of myself. And when I graduated, I presented my business idea to her father. He owned the bank in town, and I needed a loan. He told me I'd never make a living selling liquor and that I was being reckless."

He chuckles softly and shakes his head, as if he's remembering it.

"I didn't marry your mom until I was confident the business would be successful," he continues. "It's why we didn't have you until we were in our early thirties. By then, I was so absorbed with the company, with proving everyone wrong, that I didn't know any other way.

"I bought us a big house and expensive cars. I made sure neither of you ever wanted for anything, but I refused to give you both what you wanted the most ..."

"You," I whisper. "We just wanted you."

"The day she died, when we were at lunch, she asked me not to hire you," he says, tears filling his lids.

"What? Why?"

That makes no sense. She knows how hard I worked to turn my life around so I could prove to my dad that I wasn't a disappointment.

"She didn't want to lose you the way she lost me," he says softly. "I told her that it was time to cut the umbilical cord, and she got upset and left. That's the real reason why we were fighting," he admits, shocking the hell out of me. "That's why she ran out, upset. She was afraid you would become me."

"That's why you didn't ask me to come work for you," I say, the pieces finally fitting together. "You were abiding by her last wishes."

"I was," he says, "but it wasn't the right thing to do because all this time, you thought I didn't think you were capable, didn't believe you were worthy of working for Kingston or me. I never thought you were a disappointment, Anastasia. I just didn't want what happened to me to happen to you."

"So, you chose Julian as the new CEO."

"No," Julian says. "What you overheard had nothing to do with work. I was asking for your dad's permission to marry you … the right way."

"What?" I gasp. "I don't understand."

"You said you wanted a real wedding. The white dress, beautiful venue, your dad walking you down the aisle. And I want to give that to you."

He smiles softly, and my heart pounds against my rib cage. Just when I thought I couldn't love this man any more than I already do, he does something like this.

"Thank you!" I throw my arms around him as tears spill over my lids and slide down my cheeks.

"I know our engagement started off fake, but I love you, Ana, and I want to give you the world." He reaches down and presses his hand to my belly. "Both you and our baby."

I'm so caught up in the moment that it takes me a second to take in what he just said in front of my dad. When I do, I glance at him, and he's smiling.

"You didn't really think I believed your sudden engagement was real, did you?" Dad says with a laugh. "I run a successful multibillion-dollar company. I can sniff out bullshit from a mile away. I've known the entire time."

"Why didn't you say anything?" I ask, stunned at his admission.

I mean, it makes sense, but he had so many opportunities to call us out, and he didn't.

"For one, it meant having you back in my life," Dad says with a watery smile. "When I found out you were home, I didn't care how you had gotten here. But the fact that it was Julian who'd brought you home … well, maybe I'm just an old man who's in love, but that sounded a whole lot like fate to me. The man who I consider a son bringing my daughter home after six years? I couldn't have asked for anything more."

He clears his throat and smiles at both of us. "I was struggling with how to handle the CEO position. But then I got to watch the two of you fall in love, and you guys made it easy."

"What?" I ask. "How?"

"There's something you need to know, Anastasia," my dad says, his smile fading. "I don't want you to get worked up over this. Especially since you're pregnant. But I'm sick. Lung cancer. Thankfully, they caught it quickly. I already planned on retiring before I found out, but it solidifies my decision to step down. I need to focus on beating this thing, and then I want to travel and spend time with my family."

"Dad," I whisper through a choked sob.

"I'm going to be okay," he says, always so damn strong. "But I've decided to pass Kingston down to you. I want you to run our family business, sweetheart, with your husband by your side."

"But I'm pregnant," I cry, wiping the tears from my eyes.

"Which makes the childcare we're building even more essential," Julian points out. "Between you and me and our families, this baby will want for nothing." He leans in and kisses me. "We got this, Red."

Epilogue

JULIAN

ROUGHLY EIGHT MONTHS LATER

"I HATE YOU! AND IF YOU EVER COME NEAR ME AGAIN, I'm going to rip your di—"

Ana's words are cut off by her screaming as she pushes for what feels like the millionth time. She's been in labor for over forty hours. The doctor mentioned having to do a possible C-section, but our little boy just needed to come on his own time.

"You got this, Red," I tell her as she pushes through another contraction.

"I see the hair," the doctor notes. "One, maybe two more pushes, and he'll be out."

Another contraction, another push, and then he's out.

We both watch as the nurses clean him up, clearing out the fluid, and then he cries for the first time, and it's like my heart splits into two—my wife owning one half and my son owning the other.

The nurse brings him over to Ana and lays him down on her chest, and I take pictures as they both cry and bond. It's been a rough few months with Samuel's cancer taking a turn for the worse and Ana trying to remain strong for him and the company while preparing to become a mom.

But as she looks up at me with our son in her arms, I know that every hard moment led to this moment right here.

I give our little boy a kiss on his forehead, and the nurse takes a picture of the three of us and then takes him back to get him cleaned up and checked out while other nurses do the same for Ana.

About a half hour later, Ana is wheeled to recovery, and our little boy is brought in. She'd like to breastfeed for as long as she can, so the lactation specialist shows her how to latch him on, and I swear to everything, there is nothing more beautiful than watching my wife feed our son for the first time.

Without her seeing, I snap a picture of them. She might not feel beautiful right now, but one day, she'll want to see this.

After she's fed him and he's swaddled up and asleep, she asks me to bring her dad and Selene in first. When I step into the waiting room, both our families stand.

"Mom and baby are both doing great," I tell everyone. "She delivered naturally and is in recovery. He's seven pounds exactly and twenty inches." I look at

Samuel, who looks like he has aged ten years in the past eight months. "She'd like to see you first."

Since everyone knows about his health issues, nobody is surprised. Selene says she'll come soon but lets him go see Ana alone. I walk him back, and when we enter, Ana's face lights up.

He quickly washes his hands and then walks over to her bedside.

"Dad," she says through her tears, "I'd like for you to meet your grandson." She lifts our little boy and hands him to her dad while I take pictures. "Kingston Samuel Parker."

Samuel chokes out a sob at hearing his name. "Oh, Ana. He's perfect." He glances at his daughter. "Your mom would be so proud of you."

At his words, Ana breaks down in tears.

Samuel hands me Kingston and pulls his daughter into his arms.

"Thank you," he murmurs. "Thank you for coming home and giving me another chance and for giving me a precious grandson. I couldn't have asked for anything more in this life."

"No, don't say that," Ana snaps. "That sounds too much like goodbye. And us Kingstons are fighters. Besides, I still need you to walk me down the aisle."

Because she didn't want to get married while pregnant, we've planned the wedding for later this summer, and she's determined to have her dad walk her down the aisle. With her dad having lung cancer, he had to have surgery, and then there were some complications with blood clots, but now, he's doing better, and he's in the middle of getting chemo. If anyone is determined to make it through this, it's him.

"I wouldn't miss it for the world," Samuel tells her, giving her a kiss on her forehead.

After holding Kingston again, he excuses himself to go let everyone else know they can visit.

While he's gone, I sit on the edge of the bed and give Ana a kiss.

"Thank you for giving me everything I never knew I wanted," she says, her voice filled with emotion.

"You never have to thank me for loving you, Red." I give her another kiss. "This thing between us was inevitable. The moment I laid eyes on you, I was drunk on you."

She laughs and shakes her head. "You're so cheesy, Mr. Parker."

"Only for you, Mrs. Parker."

ANASTASIA
FOUR MONTHS LATER

"You look beautiful. Like a princess."

I spin around to find my dad standing in the doorway of the dressing room, dressed in a black tux, ready to walk me down the aisle. It's been three months since he finished his cancer treatment, and he's officially cancer-free. Of course, he'll have to get rechecked every so often, but right now, he's okay, and that's all that matters.

"Thank you," I choke out, my emotions getting the better of me. "And look at you." I stand and walk over to him, adjusting his bow tie so it's perfectly straight. "As handsome as ever."

"This is from your husband," he says with a chuckle, handing me a small box.

I already had his mom bring my gift over to him—a bottle of scotch I had made for him for today, along with another last-minute gift he's going to freak out over.

I open the top and find a gorgeous Tiffany bracelet nestled inside with a few charms already attached. The first one I look at is a heart-shaped locket that has *Marry Me* inscribed in the middle. On the back, it reads, *Forever drunk on you*.

I laugh at my romantically cheesy husband. My engagement ring also has the same inscription. He had it engraved before he proposed again while we were on a babymoon vacation, which he surprised me with, at the place where we fell in love—Maui.

Another one is of a heart with *Mom* engraved in the center. My heart swells. These past four months of being a mom have been the best of my life. I was so worried about failing at it, but what I didn't consider was that unlike when I isolated myself in London, here, I have family. Even my best friend, Paige, made the move to the States—after her boyfriend took a job in Houston and she moved with him—and is now working for Kingston as the new chief marketing officer.

The next charm is a crown, obviously meant to symbolize Kingston—how we met, my maiden name, and our son's name. It's sterling silver with tiny diamonds dotting the tips. It's beautiful.

And the last charm is of a champagne bottle. It's absolutely adorable. All the charms are. Julian couldn't have picked a more meaningful gift if he tried.

Under the bracelet is a note. I open it up and find Julian's chicken scratch.

Red,

Today isn't the beginning, but rather a continuation of the life we've already begun. I can't wait to marry you again, and I look forward to all the memories we'll create together.

Love,

(Jul)ian

"I love that sound," Dad says when I laugh at the way Julian signed his name. "And I love seeing you happy."

He envelops me in a hug, and I kiss his cheek.

"I'm so glad you're okay," I whisper. "And you need to stay that way." I back up and smile at him. "Especially since you're going to be a grandfather again in nine months."

Dad glances down at my stomach with wide eyes, then looks back up at me. "You're pregnant?"

"I think so," I say with a laugh. "I took a test this morning, and it came out positive. I'm going to make an appointment with the doctor once we get back from our honeymoon."

Since neither of us is anywhere near ready to leave Kingston overnight, we're keeping it simple and spending a week on the beach at a resort in Galveston.

After the wedding photographer we hired takes a few pictures of me with my dad, the wedding march begins, telling us it's go time.

The walk down the aisle is far too quick, and I choke up when my dad and Julian shake hands and hug, Julian promising to continue to love and care for me.

We say the vows we wrote for each other, and as hard as I try not to cry, I give in and let it happen when Julian surprises me with a new wedding band.

"This one has two bands interconnected," he explains. "They represent both times we've said *I do*, weaving our lives together until eternity."

He slips the band on and then puts my engagement ring back on. I stare at it for several seconds, loving that he made sure it fits perfectly with my ring.

"I did the same thing," I tell him with a watery laugh.

Since we don't have a ring bearer, Ryder, Julian's best man, is holding the ring. I take it from him and show it to Julian. The platinum wedding band is made up of two cables twisting around the entire band, symbolizing the two times we've gotten married.

"I love it," he says as I slide it onto his ring finger. "And I love you."

The officiant pronounces us husband and wife, and Julian cradles my face, then kisses me with such passion that it's as if our souls are connected, and I guess in a lot of ways that's true because this man doesn't just own my body and heart. He owns my soul too. For so long, I thought being successful would make me happy, but now, I know I was looking for happiness in all the wrong places.

But that's okay because everything happens for a reason. I had to experience the downs so I could appreciate the ups. And because of the loss I felt from losing my mom and the years I spent feeling alone, I know how precious love is. And there's no one I would rather experience it with than Julian.

"So, you're pregnant, huh?" he murmurs when we break the kiss.

I glance over at him and roll my eyes at his cocky smirk. "You're not going to be laughing when we've got two babies only a year apart."

JULIAN

"Marriage and fatherhood look good on you," my best friend, Ryder, says, clasping my shoulder. "Congrats, man."

"Thanks. And between you and me"—I lean in so no one will hear since Ana doesn't want to announce the pregnancy until she's sure and twelve weeks along—"I think Ana's pregnant again."

I waggle my brows, and Ryder chuckles.

"Better you than me," he says, shaking his head.

Ever since his marriage to Nora ended abruptly a few months back and he became a single dad, he's been struggling a bit.

"How's everything going?"

"It's rough," he says, sounding as exhausted as he looks.

"I know it's hard right now, but you did the right thing."

"I know," he agrees. "But most days, I feel like I have no idea what I'm doing."

"Trust me when I say, we all feel that way. It's not just you."

"Yeah, but at least you and Ana have each other," he says. "Anyway, enough of this depressing shit. It's your wedding day!" He grins at me. "Go dance with that beautiful wife of yours."

I glance over at Ana, who's on the dance floor, holding Kingston in her arms and twirling him around to a pop song. She nuzzles her face into his neck, blowing raspberries, and his face lights up. I can't hear him from here, but I can see him laughing. He started doing it a few days ago, and it's the most addictive sound.

"I think I'll do that," I tell Ryder.

When I reach my wife and son, they look at me with smiles.

"May I have this dance?" I ask as I pull them both into my arms.

"Always," she says.

As we dance together with Kingston in our arms and a baby growing in her belly, I can't help but think about how far we've come from the day I found her on that trophy-wife site.

Our relationship might've started out as fake, but the love we've created is real, and I wouldn't trade it for anything in the world. I wasn't kidding when I told her I was drunk on her. She's my addiction, my reason for being, and I crave her love more every day.

About the Author

Reading is like breathing in, writing is like breathing out.
– Pam Allyn

Nikki Ash resides in South Florida where she is an English teacher by day and a writer by night. When she's not writing, you can find her with a book in her hand. From the Boxcar Children, to Wuthering Heights, to the latest single parent romance, she has lived and breathed every type of book. While reading and writing are her passions, her two children are her entire world. You can probably find them at a Disney park before you would find them at home on the weekends!

Made in the USA
Monee, IL
21 August 2024

63735149R00203